AN ETHICS FOR TODAY

AN ETHICS FOR
TODAY

FINDING COMMON GROUND
BETWEEN PHILOSOPHY
AND RELIGION

RICHARD RORTY

FOREWORD BY

JEFFREY W. ROBBINS

INTRODUCTION BY

GIANNI VATTIMO

CONCLUSION BY

G. ELIJAH DANN

COLUMBIA UNIVERSITY PRESS   NEW YORK

COLUMBIA UNIVERSITY PRESS
Publishers Since 1893
New York   Chichester, West Sussex

Gianni Vattimo's introduction and Richard Rorty's lecture were transcribed
and partly translated by William McCuaig from an audio recording of
a public lecture and discussion in Turin on 21 September 2005.
Minor editorial changes have been made in both speeches.

Library of Congress Cataloging-in-Publication Data

Rorty, Richard
An ethics for today : finding common ground between philosophy
and religion / Richard Rorty ; foreword by Jeffrey W. Robbins ;
introduction by Gianni Vattimo
p. cm.
Includes bibliographical references.
ISBN 978-0-231-15056-9 (cloth: alk. paper) — ISBN 978-0-231-52543-5 (e-book)
1. Religion and ethics. 2. Catholic Church and philosophy. I. Title.

B945.R523R67 2010
170—DC22

2010014615

170
RO

CONTENTS

B.T 4/20/11

RICHARD RORTY
A PHILOSOPHICAL GUIDE TO TALKING ABOUT RELIGION

JEFFREY W. ROBBINS

Richard Rorty is famous, maybe even infamous, for his philosophical nonchalance. With his death in 2007 at the age of seventy-five, newspapers across the United States and around the world eulogized him as one of the most influential contemporary philosophers while also detailing the "casual way in which he dismissed millennia of philosophical heritage."[1] While some, such as Professor Russell Berman of Stanford University reserved an exalted place for Rorty in the pantheon of the history of philosophy by declaring that Rorty "rescued philosophy from its analytic constraints" and returned it "to core concerns of how we as a people, a country, and humanity live in a political community,"[2] Rorty himself was characteristically more muted in his self-assessment. For instance, in his brief intellectual autobiography entitled "Trotsky and the Wild Orchids" he wrote, "I have spent 40 years looking for a coherent and convincing way of formulating my worries about what, if anything, philosophy is good for."[3]

One thing that philosophy was neither good for nor good at—and indeed, the thing that Rorty spent almost the entirety of the latter half of his career cautioning against—was being the arbiter of truth. With the groundbreaking publication of *Philosophy and the Mirror of Nature* (1979), Rorty rejected not only all correspondence theories of truth but also the great swath of modern epistemology and philosophy of mind that was preoccupied with knowledge and representation. As the contemporary philosopher most credited with pushing the American tradition of pragmatism towards postmodernism, Rorty was less concerned with the truth or verifiability of a proposition than its use value. The philosopher has no exclusive access to the truth and no more clarity of understanding of the truth than the artist, scientist, politician, or shopkeeper. Thus, when asked what the mission or task of the philosopher should be, Rorty answered, "We are not here to provide principles or foundations or deep theoretical diagnoses, or a synoptic vision." What sets the philosopher apart is simply "a certain familiarity with a certain intellectual tradition, as chemists have a certain familiarity with what happens when you mix various substances together." He continued, "We are not the people to come to if you want confirmation that the things you love with all your heart are central to the structure of the universe, or that your sense of moral responsibility is 'rational and objective' rather than 'just' a result of how you were brought up."[4]

What should be discerned here is that Rorty's philosophical approach to the question of truth is part and parcel with his ethics. Just as he rejected all correspondence theories of truth, he also made clear his belief that there are no universally valid answers to moral questions. Rorty's approach here can be described as an ethics of decency and a politics of solidarity. Too often those scrambling for some universally binding ethical maxim or some objective criterion for settling decisions of right and wrong end up stumbling over themselves by their overreach, turning what should be an effort at moral suasion into either a form of coercion or obscurantism. "The main trouble," Rorty cautioned the philosopher, "is that you might succeed, and your success might let you imagine that you have something more to rely on than the tolerance and decency of your fellow human beings."[5] So when it comes to the question of "Why not be cruel?" Rorty advised the following:

> Anybody who thinks that there are well-grounded theoretical answers to this sort of question—algorithms for resolving moral dilemmas of this sort—is still, in his heart, a theologian or a metaphysician. He believes in an order beyond time and change which both determines the point of human existence and establishes a hierarchy of responsibilities.[6]

Despite their significant differences, the structure of the argument from both the theologian and the metaphysician is the same. In the case of the theologian, the argument for the good rests in a special claim to religious authority that comes by way of revealed sacred truth to which some within our religious and culturally pluralistic society subscribe and others do not. In the case of the metaphysician, moral goods derive from first truths through an almost mechanical logic, which, like the theologian's, is always and necessarily limited in its appeal because of the fundamental inability to provide any rational basis for holding certain first truths over others. In his argument against the theologian and the metaphysician, Rorty employed the technique of narrative redescription and did not so much refute their claims to special authority or insight as posit a future of human solidarity based on moral autonomy and psychological maturity. While once upon a time humanity might have needed something to worship beyond the visible world (and whether that something is literally God or, later, scientific truth makes little difference in Rorty's mind), now it is time to grow up.

By replacing the philosophical search for universally binding answers to moral questions with an appreciation for contingency, Rorty staked his hope for humanity on the prospect that we might "get to the point where we no longer worship *anything*, where we treat *nothing* as a quasi-divinity, where we treat *everything*—our language, our conscience, our community—as a product of time and chance. To reach this point, would be, in Freud's words, to 'treat chance as worthy of determining our fate.'"[7] As one scholar has summarized Rorty's basic philosophical approach, his is a philosophy "without God or his doubles."[8] So whether it is the theologian, metaphysician, or scientist, wherever and in whatever one places one's faith, know that it is only a matter of personal preference. Or as Rorty puts, "Neither reason nor experience can do much to help us decide whether to agree with Benedict XVI, or with Santayana, James, Mill, Dewey, and Habermas. There is no neutral court of appeals that will help us decide these two accounts of the human situation, both of which have inspired many acts of moral heroism." While some philosophers, scientists, and commentators (e.g., the crop of "new atheists" such as Richard Dawkins, Sam Harris, and Christopher Hitchens) might revel in the discrediting of religious beliefs, they themselves have erected a double or surrogate for God on the basis of a philosophical foundationalism that Rorty deems out of step with a postmodern sensibility wherein radical contingency goes all the way down, making it impossible to ever touch bottom, to get at truth once and for all.

While it is one thing to recognize and embrace chance in determining one's individual fate, when it comes to our common life or our politics, the attendant risks are seen by many as too dire. But here, too, Rorty was consistent. His opposition to correspondence theories of truth and moral universalism extended to his opposition to what might be termed salvational or redemptive politics. As he states:

> Relativists like myself agree that the collapse of Marxism has helped us see why politics should not try to be redemptive. But that is not because there is another sort of redemption available, the sort that Catholics believe is found in the Church. It is because redemption was a bad idea in the first place. Human beings need to be made happier, but they do not need to be redeemed, for they are not degraded beings, not immaterial souls imprisoned in material bodies, not innocent souls corrupted by original sin.

Though a strong advocate for liberal democracy, which he claimed as "the greatest achievement of our species,"[9] there are no guarantees when it comes to the common good. Separating himself from many on the political left, Rorty was quick to point out the many achievements in actualizing the egalitarian ideals of democracy. At the same time, he did not want people to make the mistake of thinking that good philosophy necessarily leads to good politics. On the contrary, "Philosophy and politics are not that tightly linked. There will always be room for a lot of philosophical disagreement between people who share the same politics, and for diametrically opposed political views among philosophers of the same school." He went further:

> It is unfortunate, I think that many people hope for a tighter link between philosophy and politics that there is or can be. In particular, people on the left keep hoping for a philosophical view which cannot be used by the political right, one which will lend itself only to good

causes. But there never will be such a view; any philosophical view is a tool which can be used by many different hands.[10]

So add here to Rorty's opposition to the theologians and metaphysicians the political ideologues who insist on an absolute uniformity of thought in order to harness political strength.

The greatness of a democratic system of governance, therefore, is not its guarantee of the actualization of its ideals but its recognition of the contingency of any political system as a work in progress. Like the deconstructionist philosopher Jacques Derrida, who always spoke of democracy as a promise to come, Rorty insisted on the limits of political philosophy and provided for a non-foundationalist thinking about democracy. In so doing, as pointed out by the democratic theorist Chantal Mouffe, both he and Derrida rejected what is perhaps the dominant strand of modern liberalism, which claims "a necessary link between universalism, rationalism and modern democracy and that constitutional democracy represents a moment in the unfolding of reason, linked to the emergence of universalist forms of law and morality."[11] By severing this link, Derrida and Rorty shared the view that "democracy does not need philosophical foundations and that it is not through rational grounding that its institutions could be made secure." In the place of this foundationalism, which in Rorty's estimation was always of limited use in shaping the political will and mobilizing the electorate, there are a "variety of practices and pragmatic moves aimed at persuading people to broaden the range of their commitments to others, to build a more inclusive community." And for Rorty in particular, "it is through sentiment and sympathy, not through rationality and universalistic moral discourse, that democratic advances take place. This is why he considers books like *Uncle*

Tom's Cabin to have played a more important role than philosophical treatises in securing moral progress."[12]

As one might expect, this last point is a sore spot among the ranks of Rorty's contemporaries in the profession of academic philosophy. In his intellectual autobiography, Rorty relates his journey from a precocious young teenager at the University of Chicago, hoping to find "a way to be both an intellectual and spiritual snob and a friend to humanity—a nerdy recluse and a fighter for justice," to his early days as an analytic philosopher pursuing the Platonic quest for certainty, to his eventual view of philosophy as one of many intellectual options. Though he does not go so far as arguing that philosophy is socially useless, he does liken it to his early incommunicable interest in wild orchids and his later literary appreciation for Proust's *Remembrance of Things Past*. So if early on he was drawn to philosophy because of its apparent promise—in the words of Yeats, to "hold reality and justice in a single vision," or in the words of Rorty, "to reconcile Trotsky and the orchids"—he later was instrumental in redefining both the purpose and status of philosophy. As he wrote in *Philosophy and the Mirror of Nature*, "The abandonment of the image of the Mirror leads us to abandon the notion of philosophy as a discipline which adjudicates the claims of science and religion, mathematics and poetry, reason and sentiment, allocating an appropriate place to each."[13]

While some literary critics during this period were speaking of the death of the author and some theologians of the death of God, Rorty was making the case for the end of philosophy as we know it. No longer could it be conceived as a super-science, but instead it had become the "bedfellow of *literary* culture."[14] Its function was not to arbitrate truth but to tell stories. With doing philosophy, like telling stories, there is a "shared ability to appreciate the power of redescribing, the power of language to make new and different things possible and important."[15] In this sense, Rorty insisted, "Interesting philosophy is rarely an examination of the pros and cons of a thesis. Usually it is, implicitly or explicitly, a contest between an entrenched vocabulary which has become a nuisance and a half-formed new vocabulary which vaguely promises new things."[16] Or, as he concludes:

> As relativists like myself see the matter, the struggle between relativism and fundamentalism is between two great products of the human imagination. It is not a contest between a view that corresponds to reality and one that does not. It is between two visionary poems. One offers a vision of vertical ascent toward something greater than the merely human; the other offers a vision of horizontal progress toward a planetwide cooperative commonwealth.

With this transformation in the self-understanding of philosophy's function came a loss in its preeminent status—a demotion welcomed by Rorty but that, needless to say, did not sit well with many of his colleagues.

This change in both the function and status of philosophy is captured quite well by Neil Gross in his interesting study of Rorty, which aims to use Rorty as a case study in developing the new sociology of ideas. Gross begins by contrasting an early Rorty article published in 1965 to one that came out seventeen years later. In the older article, published while he was still housed within the philosophy department at Princeton University, Rorty defended a position that had been advanced by the Australian philosopher J. J. C. Smart on "identity theory." The article is very technical and aimed only at specialists within the field. In the 1982 article, published after Rorty had been named the Kenan Professor of the Humanities at the University of

Virginia, he surveys contemporary American philosophy in the form of a story of the demise of logical positivism. In contrast to the earlier article, the later article was written for a general audience. So while the first was a textbook case of a work in analytic philosophy written by and for a specialist within the profession, the second was postanalytic. As Gross writes:

> Years earlier he had been a hard-nosed analyst himself, engaged in rarefied debates in the philosophy of mind. Now he encouraged his fellow philosophers to take a 'relaxed attitude' toward the question of logical rigor, to stop drawing arbitrary boundaries between philosophy and other humanities fields, to open up more to the history of philosophy, to put the social and political concerns raised by Continental philosophers back on the table, and to cease worrying whether philosophy has a coherent paradigm.[17]

As Gross argues, this "relaxed attitude" was hard earned by Rorty, and to a degree, at least, reflects a paradigmatic case of self-invention that makes Rorty into the quintessential American philosopher. It grew out of a certain dissatisfaction with what Rorty perceived to be the constrictions of analytic philosophy, but also a disillusionment with the profession of academia and a desire to engage in thinking that mattered by truly engaging the concrete sociopolitical problems of the day.

The irony is that the more Rorty distanced himself from the profession of academic philosophy (e.g., leaving his post in the philosophy department at Princeton University to become a Professor of Humanities at Virginia, publishing more and more articles in newspapers and magazines than in traditional scholarly journals, and so on), the more influential as a philosopher he became.[18] And, as Gross adds, "Perhaps the true measure of Rorty's fame—or infamy—however, was that he managed to cross over, escaping the confines of academic discourse and entering popular culture, where he became a whipping boy for conservatives eager to denounce academic and leftist excess."[19]

Rorty would add to this that he was the target of ire not only from the conservatives on the right but also those on the left of the ideological and political spectrum. For every David Brooks (who proclaimed that "while this stuff appears radical, if you strip away Rorty's grand declarations about the death of God and Truth and get down to the type of public personality that Rorty calls for, he begins to appear instead as the Norman Rockwell for the intellectual bourgeoisie in the age of the booming stock market")[20] or Allan Bloom (who once wrote that Rorty had "given up on America"),[21] there were those on the left such as the Yale political philosopher Sheldon Wolin or the British Marxist thinker Terry Eagleton who saw in Rorty the chief philosopher of the "leisured, cultured elite."[22] As Rorty described the situation, "The left's favourite word for me is 'complacent', just as the right's is 'irresponsible.'"[23] He admitted that the criticism hurt, primarily because it seemed to presume that Rorty had come to his respective positions on philosophy, ethics, and politics for frivolous reasons.

Relaxed, even nonchalant perhaps, but frivolous Rorty was not. By spending over forty years worrying about what philosophy was good for, Rorty has been good for philosophy. By standing above and outside the fray of the technical squabbles and turf battles among the professionals, he has managed to reorient philosophy's self-understanding of its primary task, all the while speaking directly to a public that has little taste and little patience—but much need—for philosophical reflection. Nowhere is that more evident than in this short book. As America's last and best-known public philosopher, no one among his contemporaries was better equipped to write an ethics for the layperson. And it is here, when contrasting such potentially inflammatory and little understood topics as fundamentalism and relativism, that the many advantages of his philosophical nonchalance are revealed.

But first, before turning directly to the brief text that will follow, a word must be said about Rorty's views on religion. Reference has already been made to his basic acceptance of the proposition of the death of God. This should come as hardly a surprise given his upbringing in a home where "The Case for Leon Trotsky" occupied the place of reverence reserved for the Bible in most other homes. As Rorty himself put, he was raised "knowing that all decent people were, if not Trotskyites, at least socialists."[24] Though a staunch secularist, he was not militant or dogmatic in his atheism. On the contrary, as Danny Postel suggests in a magazine article for *New Humanist*, Rorty is probably best described as a "boring atheist."[25] That is to say, for Rorty religious claims simply did not register as a serious matter of philosophical dispute requiring much intellectual energy. Of course he recognized that religious belief had contributed greatly to the development of human civilization in the past, but it was his belief that we had "cobbled together, in the course of the last two hundred years, a specifically secularist moral tradition—one that regards the free consensus of the citizens of a democratic society, rather than the Divine Will, as the source of moral imperatives."[26] In the terminology of his pragmatist predecessor William James, religious belief was simply not a "live option" for Rorty. People are free to believe what they will, but as a secularist, he was committed to drawing a sharp line drawn between church and state and between personal conscience and public policy.

It is precisely with this commitment, predicated as it was on the private-public split, that Rorty left himself open to criticism.[27] For instance, when he famously described religion as a "conversation-stopper," he was being consistent in his philosophical nonchalance to a subject that inflames, mobilizes, and is cherished by so many, but it was a nonchalance that bordered on the flippant.[28] As has become increasingly evident, especially in the post-9/11 context, religion might very well be a conversation-stopper, but there is no value in making a virtue out of this necessity. We had better learn to talk about religion. Not only does the alternative mean a narrowing of our political discourse and an abstraction of our philosophical reflection—two tendencies that Rorty long fought against—but also by learning to talk about, and in spite of, our religious differences (which certainly includes the religious option of unbelief as well), we might hope to avoid the violence and dehumanization that otherwise might be allowed to go unchecked, untested, and hidden from the light of day. By seeking to exclude religion from our political discourse because it is not something that the entire public shares, Rorty is actually guilty of the very thing of which he accuses religion—namely, cutting the conversation short. As the moral philosopher Jeffrey Stout writes, "Reasons actually held in common do not get us far enough toward answers to enough of our political questions. The proposed policy of restraint, if adopted, would cause too much silence at precisely the points where more discussion is most badly needed. The policy would itself be a conversation-stopper."[29]

Rorty is certainly not alone among contemporary philosophers in his adoption of this strict secularist stance. In fact, this has been the norm among mainstream modern philosophers in the liberal tradition, as reflected in the work of John Rawls and Jürgen Habermas as well. This insistence that religion remain a private matter does not necessarily betray a philosophical hostility to religion or even a devaluing of religion. Instead, it expresses an ultimate commitment to the importance of liberty and freedom of conscience. Nevertheless, while Rawls has remained firm in this secularist stance, Habermas has reconsidered his views. While he still describes his philosophical approach as one of methodological atheism, he has cautioned that excluding religious discourse entirely from politics would deprive "secular society from important resources of meaning."[30] In addition, he has urged a change in the secularist self-understanding of the modern state: "The liberal state must not transform the requisite institutional separation of religion and politics into an undue mental or psychological burden for those of its citizens who follow a faith."[31]

In this way, Habermas has made the transition from a secularist to a postsecularist understanding of the proper relationship between religion and politics.[32] Religion may very well be a personal matter, but that does not mean that it must be confined to the realm of the private and left without any public, or political, consequence. And it seems that even Rorty was at least gesturing toward the same in the public dialogue that that forms the heart of this book when, immediately after insisting on the secular being the political norm, he goes on to say, "Let us give up even secular ways of trying to assure ourselves that there is something large and powerful on our side. Let us try to make progress simply through hope for cooperation with one another, rather than in hope of achieving universal truth or contact with the transcendent." The point, after all, as Rorty reiterates in the answer that follows, is that society is "constantly attempting to make the future still more different from the past."

In his distinction between relativism and fundamentalism, Rorty characterizes relativists as those who believe that "Being open to doctrinal change . . . is the only way to avoid the evils of the past." Rorty's iconoclastic philosophy has effectively smashed the idols of theology, metaphysics, ethics, and politics, offering a series of successive rejections of their various false starts and false paths. As he insists, this does not mean that we are any closer to the truth or in closer proximity to the transcendent. Instead, more modestly, it simply means we are "more experienced, more able to see what will cause harm and what might do good." Therefore, to those who have lodged their complaint about the modern reign of secular reason, even on this point where Rorty most firmly held his ground by remaining a staunch secularist to the end, he may yet still prove to be an ally. After all, what he models here is a way of having a public conversation about religion—indeed, about fundamental religious differences. This book, therefore, does not mark the conversation's end, but its beginning.

NOTES

1   *The Times* (London), June 12, 2007, http://www.timesonline.co.uk/tol/comment/obituaries/article1917517.ece.

2   Quoted in Patricia Cohen, "Richard Rorty, Philosopher, Dies at 75," *New York Times*, June 11, 2007, http://www.nytimes.com/2007/06/11/obituaries/11rorty.html.

3   Richard Rorty, *Philosophy and Social Hope* (New York: Penguin Books, 1994), 11.

4   Ibid., 19–20.

5   Ibid., 20.

6   Rorty, *Contingency, Irony, and Solidarity* (Cambridge: Cambridge University Press, 1989), xv.

7   Ibid., 22; emphasis his.

8   See D. Vaden House, *Without God or His Doubles: Realism, Relativism, and Rorty* (New York: Brill, 1994).

9   Rorty, *Philosophy and Social Hope*, 20.

10 Ibid., 23.

11 Chantal Mouffe, "Deconstruction, Pragmatism, and the Politics of De-mocracy," in *Deconstruction and Pragmatism* (New York: Routledge, 1996), 1.

12 Ibid., 1, 5.

13 Rorty, *Philosophy and the Mirror of Nature* (Princeton, N.J.: Princeton University Press, 1979), 212.

14 See Bruce Silver and Nancy Stanlick, *Philosophy in America: Interpretive Essays*, vol. 2 (Englewood Cliffs, N.J.: Prentice Hall, 2004), 213.

15 Rorty, *Contingency, Irony, and Solidarity*, 39.

16 Ibid., 9.

17 Neil Gross, *Richard Rorty: The Making of an American Philosopher* (Chicago: University of Chicago Press, 2008), 4.

18 For instance, Gross counts more than 2,000 citations to *Philosophy and the Mirror of Nature* in the Arts and Humanities Citation Index and more than 50 humanities articles published each year with the keyword "Rorty" throughout the 1990s.

19 Ibid., 25.

20 David Brooks, "Achieving Richard Rorty: Leftist Thought in Middle-Class America," *The Weekly Standard*, June 1, 1998, 31.

21 Quoted in Rorty, *Philosophy and Social Hope*, 3.

22 Ibid.

23 Ibid., 4.

24 Ibid., 6.

25 See Danny Postel, "High Flyer: Richard Rorty Obituary," *New Humanist* 122, no. 4 (July/August 2007).

26 See Danny Postel, "Last Words from Richard Rorty," *The Progressive* (June 2007): http://www.progressive.org/mag_postel0607.

27 See especially Jeffrey Stout, *Democracy and Tradition* (Princeton, N.J.: Princeton University Press, 2004). As Stout writes in contradistinction

to Rorty, "I came of age ethically, politically, and spiritually in the Civil Rights movement, where I acquired my democratic commitments from prophetic ministers. In college, when I moved rapidly down the path that leads from Schleiermacher to Feuerbach, Emerson, and beyond, I found myself collaborating mainly with dissenting Protestants, secular Jews, and members of the radical Catholic underground in the struggle against U.S. involvement in the Vietnam War. I have known since then that it is possible to build democratic coalitions including people who differ religiously and to explore those differences deeply and respectfully without losing one's integrity as a critical intellect. This book is offered in the hope that similarly diverse coalitions and equally full expression of differences remain possible in democratic culture today, if we can only summon the will to form them" (91).

28 See Rorty, *Philosophy and Social Hope*, 168–174.

29 Stout, *Democracy and Tradition*, 89–90.

30 Jürgen Habermas, *The Future of Human Nature* (New York: Polity, 2003), 109.

31 Ibid., 9.

32 For a discussion of theopolitical ramifications of this broad cultural shift to the postsecular, see *Political Theologies: Public Religions in a Post-Secular World*, ed. Hent de Vries and Lawrence E. Sullivan (New York: Fordham University Press, 2006).

AN ETHICS FOR TODAY

INTRODUCTION

GIANNI VATTIMO

I made the acquaintance of Richard Rorty at Milwaukee in 1979, where they had organized a conference on postmodernism. Those taking part included the late Ihab Hassan, an Egyptian thinker who had written books on postmodernity; Hans-Georg Gadamer; and Rorty. I was a touch diffident vis-à-vis Rorty because, as well as being older than I, though not by much, he had just won an important prize for his book *Philosophy and the Mirror of Nature*, and that made him the featured American philosopher at the conference. He was very kind, though, and after taking a quick look at my paper, he said he wanted to read it; I hadn't read his book, which had only come out that year, any more than he had read any of mine, but we realized we were both saying much the same thing. From that moment a strong friendship arose, and on my part a certain devoted respect as well.

Why did we find this level of understanding right from the start? It had something to do with the presence of Hans-Georg Gadamer, the master of twentieth-century hermeneutics, who died in 2002 at the age of 101, and who was healthy all his life. The origin of this meeting of minds with Rorty was tied to the fact that Rorty by then was already anticipating what later became known as the postanalytic current in Anglo-American philosophy, with his idea—which I will try to state briefly, to give you an idea of the direction of his work—that the three great thinkers of the twentieth century had been John Dewey, Ludwig Wittgenstein, and Martin Heidegger. Now, if linking Dewey to Wittgenstein were not audacious enough, to add Heidegger and make it a threesome was certainly scandalous. But also creative. American philosophy in the years that followed did not entirely mutate into a form of hermeneutic pragmatism, but there was undeniably a rapprochement (I have in mind many eminent figures, like Robert Brandom, well known today in Europe) with certain strands of European philosophy inspired fundamentally by hermeneutics.

I'll spare you a lecture on hermeneutics, but to put it in a nutshell: twentieth-century philosophy had once cherished a dream of becoming a rigorous science, a dream that (on either side of the English Channel, if not the Atlantic) had characterized positivism and phenomenology, respectively. But as Husserl put it, the dream was "dreamed out" (*ausgeträumt*), it faded away, and with it the idea that philosophy ought to be a robust representation either of reality or, at any rate, of the modes in which we represent reality.

Rorty's book, of which he gave me a copy in Milwaukee, came out in Italian a few years later under the title *La filosofia e lo specchio della natura* (Bompiani, 1986), with an introduction cowritten by me and an authoritative Wittgensteinian colleague, Diego Marconi. What it says in substance is that for many centuries philosophy had busied itself with furnishing guarantees that the way we represent reality to ourselves is reliable. The term "mirror" signified that philosophy was supposed to help us to reflect Nature faithfully, either by giving guidance to science, as Kant would have it, or else by simply revealing the basic structures allowing us to mirror Nature.

But for Rorty all this was really no more than what Heidegger had called it, a metaphysical reverie: it was the idea that the essence of our being in the world consisted in contemplating the objective truth and then, above all, observing it. The point is that "observe" in English, like "*osservare*" in Italian, can signify both to inspect something to see how it works and also to comply with or follow it, as when we observe a law. The European metaphysical tradition was, if you like, tied to the idea that, in observing how things are, one learns to observe norms as well.

Norms, however, as Hume (himself a British philosopher) said, cannot be derived from facts. If a person is something, that is what he is. If he isn't, and is told that he must be, then that imperative has to be justified. "Be a man!" is what you generally hear from those who want to send you off to war, but you are owed an explanation as to why you have to go to war.

Why does Rorty's discourse refer to great authors such as Wittgenstein, and Dewey above all? Because Dewey is the founder of pragmatism. Rorty takes up pragmatism in light of Wittgenstein, who in the second period of his thought had invented linguistic games: every sector of our existence speaks an idiom, and the truth or falsity, or at any rate the reasonableness, of a proposition, depends on the rules of the idiom in which it is enunciated. It's like what we say in Italian: "coi santi in chiesa, coi fanti in taverna." If you start singing hymns to the Virgin Mary in the tavern the lads will probably laugh you out of the place, just like churchgoers will chase you out of their place if you start singing tavern songs there.

So Rorty's stance imposed a different horizon on the problem of observational truth: no longer that of inspecting how things are but that of operating in (and on) reality. Pragmatism doesn't mean just "what is true is what works" but also "we are in the world not to inspect how things are, but to produce, to make, to transform reality." Toward what end? Toward our happiness. Are we meant to feel happy when we have ascertained how things are? Why would we? If someone is ill and is told that she is ill because she has a wasting disease, will she feel happy? No, unless you also give her the drug that will cure her. In that circumstance, knowing the truth serves a purpose, the purpose of trying not to be too unhappy. So much for a shorthand description of Richard Rorty's pragmatic stance.

Where is the convergence with hermeneutic philosophers and Heidegger? Heidegger was also the one who said that existence is a project and that every philosophy—every claim not so much to truth as to validity—is grounded in the shareability of the project it presents. I myself have grown lazy, and I no longer even pick up philosophical works claiming to tell me how things are: only ones that declare at the outset how they want to make them become. If a book sets out a project, then it interests me, if not then I might read it because I have to review it, but certainly not because I am curious to know how matters stand according to that particular book.

I would sum up Rorty's stance—which I portray a little differently than he would himself—by referring to a book we published together, *The Future of Religion* (Columbia University Press, 2005). In the twentieth century, philosophy advanced from the idea of truth to the idea of charity: the highest value is not truth as objective description; the highest value is accord with others. To this, some object: "How are we to reach accord if we don't know how things are?" I say that we know how things are when we have reached accord, in other words when, on the basis of a set of premises, needs, and methods that we share, passed down to us by history, we get to a point at which we agree, we are satisfied, we are no longer flinging the question "What on earth do you mean by that?" at one another.

This is my way of stating that Rorty and many of his own masters are right, that our common friend Gadamer was right, that in many respects even the late Jacques Derrida (a close friend of Rorty) was right, and Jürgen Habermas, too. Although Habermas has recently begun talking about human nature, winning applause from the Vatican hierarchy (on that specific point anyway), he actually thinks that the rationality of a discourse consists in its being decently presentable to others. I would never say things here tonight that you would find less than decent. Then we can go ahead and debate them and probe them. But the essential point, once again, is not so much their correspondence to the factual data—the mirror of Nature—as the common search for happiness, for accord, and also, if you will, for charity.

Ladies and gentlemen, I give you Richard Rorty.

AN ETHICS FOR TODAY

RICHARD RORTY

I'm very grateful to Gianni Vattimo for his sympathetic remarks about my philosophical writings, and I'm very grateful to Antonella Parigi and her colleagues in Torino Spiritualità for inviting me on this occasion. I have been in Torino before, but this is the first time I have been in the Teatro Regio, and it is a very impressive stage from which to speak. My topic today is spirituality and secularism. Pope Benedict XVI has complained that it is becoming very difficult for the Church to say what it believes. Very soon, the pope has written, one will not be able to affirm that homosexuality constitutes, as the Catholic Church teaches, an objective disorder in the structure of human existence. The pope's prediction may well come true. Where I come from, on the campus of my university, it is already the case that to condemn homosexuality or to treat homosexuality, homosexual desire, as perverse or somehow immoral would be regarded as an outrageous display of vicious intolerance. So the pope is justified in fearing that the pressure of outraged public opinion may force the Church to pass over the topic of homosexuality in silence. I hope that this will happen. I hope that the pope's fears will be confirmed because I think that condemning homosexuality has produced a great deal of unnecessary, pointless human misery. The Church's attitude has greatly decreased the sum of human happiness. The controversy about homosexuality raises a central question about the nature of morality. Is the Church right that there is such a thing as the structure of human existence, which can serve as a moral reference point? Or, do we human beings have no moral obligations except helping one another satisfy our desires, thus achieving the greatest possible amount of happiness? I agree with John Stuart Mill, the great utilitarian philosopher, that that is the only moral obligation we have.

The Church, of course, holds that views such as Mill's reduce human beings to the level of animals. But philosophers like me think that utilitarianism exalts us by offering us a challenging moral ideal. Utilitarianism leads to heroic and self-sacrificing efforts on behalf of social justice. Such efforts are entirely compatible with the claim that there is no such thing as the structure of human existence. The Spanish philosopher George Santayana once said that superstition is the confusion of an ideal with power. Superstition, he said is the belief that any legitimate ideal must somehow be grounded in something already actual, something transcendent that sets this ideal before us. What the pope calls the structure of human existence is an example of such a transcendent entity. Santayana said, and I agree, that the only source of moral ideals is the human imagination. Santayana hoped that human beings would eventually give up the idea that moral ideals must be grounded in something larger than ourselves. He hoped that we would come to think of all such ideals as human creations and none the worse for that. Santayana's claim that imagination is a good enough source for the ideal led him to say that religion and poetry are identical in essence. He used the term "poetry" in an expansive sense to mean something like "product of the imagination." He used the word "religion" in an equally large sense to include political idealism, aspirations to make the life of a community radically different, radically better than it had been before. Poetry, Santayana said, is called religion when it intervenes in life, and religion when it merely supervenes upon life is seen to be nothing but poetry. Neither poetry nor religion, Santayana believed, should be thought of as telling us about something that is already real. We should stop asking about the claims made on us by an ideal, nor should we ask about the nature of our obligation to live up to the ideal. To give oneself over to a moral ideal is like giving oneself over to another human being. When we fall in love with another person, we do not ask about the source or the nature of our obligation to cherish that person's welfare. It is equally pointless to do so when we have fallen in love with an ideal. Most of Western philosophy is, like Christian theology, an attempt to get in touch with something larger than ourselves. So to accept Santayana's view, as I do, is to repudiate the tradition that Heidegger called ontotheology. That repudiation means ceasing to ask both metaphysical questions about the ground or the source of our ideals and epistemological questions about how one can be certain that one has chosen the correct ideal. To recur to my previous analogy, it is silly to ask for a proof that those whom we love are the best possible people for us to have fallen in love with. But of course we can fall out of love with one person as a result of falling in love with another person. Similarly, we may desert one ideal because we have come to cherish another ideal. What we cannot do is to choose between two people, or between two ideals, by reference to neutral criteria. When it is a matter, for example, of conversion from an atheistic form of spirituality to a religious form, or from a religious form to an atheistic form, it is futile to look for a demonstration that one has turned in the right direction. The onto-theological tradition that Santayana stigmatized as superstition insists, however, that one must raise metaphysical and epistemological questions about our ideals, that it is our duty to follow in Plato's footsteps. The way of thinking that began with Socrates and Plato tells us that simply to throw oneself into the realization of a project is to become a creature of blind will, bestial rather than human. Calling that project the realization of an ideal does not make such unthinking willfulness any better. This Platonic way of thinking finds expression in one of the new pope's most frequently quoted remarks. In a homily given just before his election to the papacy, Cardinal Ratzinger said:

> Today, having a clear faith based on the creed of Christ, the creed of the Church, is often labeled fundamentalism, whereas relativism—that is, letting oneself be tossed here and there, carried about by every wind of doctrine—seems the only attitude that can cope with modern times. We are building a dictatorship of relativism that does not recognize anything as definitive and whose ultimate goal consists solely of one's own ego and its desires.

Philosophers like Santayana and Mill do indeed refuse to recognize anything as definitive. This is because they think that every reported object of philosophical speculation or of religious worship is a product of the human imagination. Someday it may be replaced by a better object. There is no destined end to this process of replacement, no point at which we can claim to have found the correct ideal once and for all. There is nothing already in existence to which our moral convictions should try to correspond. What the pope disparagingly calls the relativists' habit of being carried about by every wind of doctrine is viewed by philosophers like myself as openness to new possibilities, willingness to consider all suggestions about what might increase human happiness. Being open to doctrinal change, we believe, is the only way to avoid the evils of the past.

So far I have been outlining the controversy between these two opposing views about the nature of morality. Now I would like to focus on the terms "fundamentalism" and "relativism." Both of these words are frequently used as pejoratives. Fundamentalism is often used to refer to an absurdly uncritical invocation of scriptural texts. But no one could accuse a sophisticated theologian like Benedict XVI of this. Relativism is often used to refer to the absurd thesis that every moral conviction is as good as every other moral conviction. But that is a thesis no philosopher has ever tried to defend. One can, however, give a useful, respectable sense to the word "fundamentalism" by using it simply to designate the view that ideals are valid only when grounded in reality. This is the view put forward by the Church. One can give a respectable and useful sense to "relativism" by defining it simply as the denial of fundamentalism. Relativists on this definition are those who believe that we would be better off without such notions as unconditional moral obligations grounded in the structure of human existence. In an essay the pope wrote in 1996, when he was still Cardinal Ratzinger, he wrote: "Relativism appears to be the philosophical foundation of democracy." He continued by saying "relativist philosophers define their doctrine positively on the basis of the concepts of tolerance, dialectic, epistemology, and freedom, freedom which would be limited by maintaining one truth as being valid for everyone." The cardinal summarized the relativists' line of argument as follows: "Democracy is said to be founded on no one's being able to claim to know the right way forward. It draws life from all the ways acknowledging each other as fragmentary attempts at improvement and trying to agree in common through dialogue. A free society is said to be a relativistic society. Only on this condition can it remain free and open-ended."

The philosophical attitude that the cardinal described in this passage is shared by John Stuart Mill, John Dewey, and Jürgen Habermas. These three philosophers all suggest that we think of truth as what wins out in the free market of ideas rather than as correspondence to an antecedent reality. This is the view that Gianni Vattimo summarized in his introductory remarks. All these philosophers think of democratic societies as founded on the idea that nothing is sacred because everything is up for discussion. In the essay from which I quoted, Cardinal Ratzinger conceded that relativism is not without intellectual resources. He admitted that it cannot be dismissed out of hand. In words that might have scandalized Pius IX, the future Benedict XVI wrote as follows:

> In the area of politics this relativist view is to a great extent true. The one single political opinion does not exist. What is relative, the construction of a freely ordered common life for men, cannot be absolute. Thinking that it could be was precisely the error of Marxism and of the political theologies. But even in the realm of politics, one cannot always manage with absolute relativism. There are things that are wrong and can never become right. Killing innocent people for instance, denying individuals the right to be treated as humans, and to a way of life appropriate to them. There are things that are right and can never become wrong. In the realm of politics and society, therefore, one cannot deny relativism a certain right. The problem is based on the fact that relativism sees itself as being unlimited.

The cardinal went on to argue that the need for limits to relativism shows that: "Wherever politics tries to be redemptive, it is promising too much. Where politics wishes to do the work of God, it becomes not divine but diabolical."

Relativists like myself agree that the collapse of Marxism has helped us see why politics should not try to be redemptive. But that is not because there is another sort of redemption available, the sort that Catholics believe is found in the Church. It is because redemption was a bad idea in the first place. Human beings need to be made happier, but they do not need to be redeemed, for they are not degraded beings, not immaterial souls imprisoned in material bodies, not innocent souls corrupted by original sin. They are, as Nietzsche put it, clever animals, clever because they, unlike the other animals, have learned how to cooperate with one another in order better to fulfill one another's desires. In the course of history, we clever animals have acquired new desires, and we have become quite different from our animal ancestors. For our cleverness has not only enabled us to adjust means to ends, it has enabled us to imagine new ends, to dream up new ideals. Nietzsche, when he described the effects of the cooling-off of the sun, wrote: "And so the clever animals had to die." He would have done better to have written: "And so the brave, imaginative, idealistic, self-improving animals had to die." The notion of redemption presupposes a distinction between the lower, mortal, animal parts of the soul, and the higher, spiritual, immortal part. Redemption is what would occur when the higher finally triumphs over the lower, when reason conquers passion, or when grace defeats sin. In much of the onto-theological tradition, the lower-higher distinction is construed as a distinction between the part that is content with finitude and the part that yearns for the infinite.

At the end of the essay from which I have been quoting, Cardinal Ratzinger wrote that:

> The reason faith still has a chance is that it corresponds to the nature of man. Man is more generously proportioned than the way Kant and the various post-Kantian philosophies see him, or will allow him to be. The longing for the infinite is alive and unquenchable within man. So only the God who himself became finite in order to tear apart our finitude, and lead us out into the wide spaces of his infinity can redeem us.

Plato founded the tradition to which the pope adheres by connecting the idea of immortality with that of immateriality and infinity. The immaterial soul, whose true home is the immaterial world, will someday inhabit the wide spaces of its own infinity. It will achieve immunity to the disasters that inevitably overtake any merely spatio-temporal, merely finite being. It is often said that those who, like myself and the other philosophers to whom I have referred, those who disagree with Plato, lack any sense of the spiritual. If spirituality is defined as a yearning for the infinite, then this charge is perfectly justified.

But if spirituality is thought of as an exalted sense of new possibilities opening up for finite beings, it is not. The difference between these two meanings of the term spirituality is the difference between the hope to transcend finitude and the hope for a world in which human beings live far happier lives than they live at the present time. Ancient materialists like Epicurus lacked this kind of hope. They were incapable of this kind of moral idealism, incapable of the spiritual elevation that became possible for secularist Europeans and Americans after the democratic revolutions of the eighteenth century. Since that time a form of spirituality has emerged that turns away from the possibility of sainthood, turns away from perfecting an individual human life, toward the possibility of perfecting human society. Though largely Christian in its original inspiration, the political idealism of modern times has no need or use for the idea that there is something over and above what Cardinal Ratzinger called "the ego and its desires." Not just my ego but the egos of all human beings. The difference between the two views of morality that I have been discussing in these remarks is well illustrated by the contrast between the pope's dismissive reference to "the ego and its desires," and my favorite passage in the writings of the American philosopher William James. James wrote as follows: "Every de facto claim creates insofar forth an obligation. Take any demand however slight which any creature, however weak, may make. Ought it not for its own sole sake to be satisfied? If not, prove why not. The only possible kind of proof you could adduce would be the exhibition of another creature who should make a demand that went the other way."

For Mill, James, Dewey, Habermas, and the other philosophers of social democracy, the answer to the question "Are some human desires bad?" is: No, but some desires do get in the way of our project of maximizing the overall satisfaction of desire. For example, my desire that my children should have more to eat than my neighbor's children is not intrinsically evil. But this desire should not be fulfilled. There is no such thing as intrinsically evil desire. There are only desires that must be subordinated to other desires in the interests of fairness. For those who adopt the utilitarian ideal of maximizing happiness, moral progress consists in enlarging the range of those whose desires are taken into account. It is a matter of what the contemporary American philosopher Peter Singer calls "enlarging the circle of the 'we,'" enlarging the number of people whom we think of as "one of us." The most salient example of this enlargement is the change that took place when the rich began to think of the poor as fellow citizens rather than as people whose station in life had been ordained by God. The rich had to stop thinking that the least advantaged children were somehow meant to lead less happy lives than those of their own children. Only then could they start thinking about wealth and poverty as mutable social institutions rather than as parts of an immutable order. Another obvious example of enlarging the circle of the "we" is the recent partial but encouraging success of feminism. The males have recently been more willing to put themselves in the shoes of the females. Still another example is the greater willingness of heterosexuals to put themselves in the shoes of homosexuals, to imagine what it must be like to be told that the love they feel for another person is a disgusting perversion.

I shall end by confronting the question of how one goes about deciding between James's view that any desire has a right to be fulfilled, if it does not interfere with the fulfillment of other desires, and those who regard certain desires and acts as intrinsically evil. How should one decide between those who find, for example, the prohibition of sodomy as absurd as the prohibition against eating shellfish, and those who believe sodomy to be an objective disorder in the structure of human existence? Philosophers of my persuasion do not believe that simply by taking thought, simply by engaging in philosophical reflection, we can resolve issues such as this. As we see it, Mill has one vision of an ideal society, and the pope has another. We cannot decide between these two visions on the basis of philosophical principles because our choice between alternative principles is determined by our preferences between possible futures for humanity. Philosophy is not a restraint on the use of the imagination; it is one more product of the imagination. History is of no more help than philosophy, for history can be read in too many different ways. In many of his writings, the pope has suggested that the need to conceive of moral obligations as imposed by an eternally fixed moral law has been shown by our historical experience with fascism and communism. But of course his opponents cite the horrors committed by the Catholic Church to argue for the opposite conclusion. Whereas the pope accuses relativism of leading to Auschwitz and the gulag, his opponents accuse fundamentalism of excusing the practice of burning homosexuals alive. If one thinks of philosophy as an appeal to reason and of history as an appeal to experience, then I can sum up what I have said by saying that neither reason nor experience can do much to help us decide whether to agree with Benedict XVI or with Santayana, James, Mill, Dewey, and Habermas. There is no neutral court of appeal that will help us decide between these two accounts of the human situation, both of which have inspired many acts of moral heroism. In the pope's vision, humans must remain faithful to what he calls "the common human experience of contact with a truth that is greater than we are." In the relativist vision, there never was, and never will be, a truth that is greater than we are. The very idea of such a truth is a confusion of ideals with power. As relativists like myself see the matter, the struggle between relativism and fundamentalism is between two great products of the human imagination. It is not a contest between a view that corresponds to reality and one that does not. It is between two visionary poems. One offers a vision of vertical ascent toward something greater than the merely human; the other offers a vision of horizontal progress toward a planetwide cooperative commonwealth. Thank you very much.

GIANNI VATTIMO   There must be an absolutist or anti-relativist in the hall.

A MEMBER OF THE AUDIENCE The problem that concerns me is whether mysticism is absolutely to be excluded from your way of thinking, or not. The real sense of mysticism, I mean something transcendental—does it exist or not in your vision?

RICHARD RORTY I think that the mystics, like the poets, are among the great imaginative geniuses who have helped human moral and intellectual progress. Where I think we disagree is on the question of whether the mystical must be a way of putting us in touch with the transcendent. As I see it, mystical experience is a way of leaping over the boundaries of the language one speaks. Leaps over those boundaries lead to the creation of new language. And the creation of new language leads to intellectual and moral progress.

A MEMBER OF THE AUDIENCE Vattimo was asking whether there was an absolutist in the room. I don't want to defend an absolutist position a priori, but I do wish to put a couple of questions, because, while it is true that using the word "relativism" to cover a whole range of positions amounts to oversimplification, the converse is also true: using the word "absolutism" is also an oversimplification, for example to characterize things said by Ratzinger.

But I would like to put a couple of question, one political, the other historiographical. Since Richard Rorty is American, I would ask him this: in the United States today, what political stance could be described as free of absolutism? Because American democracy presents itself as prior to philosophy, above and beyond philosophy, and I think there is no affirmation more absolutist than that. As I see it, democracy isn't, and can't claim to be, anything more than just one entirely transitory form of civilization. But in the United States that idea is not accepted, and the United States doesn't want it accepted in Europe, or the Middle East, or the rest of the world either. Who is more absolutist here? Ratzinger, or this conception? I think it is this American conception, not Ratzinger. Where does Professor Rorty stand on this question?

Second, a question about history: is it possible to renounce objectivity altogether? I understand that it is something we must always strive for without ever attaining. But one gets the feeling that, in a stance like yours, there is an a priori renunciation of objectivity. Hence history and historiography becomes just an expression of the imagination and the will to power, always and everywhere.

RICHARD RORTY The reason that I did not contrast relativism and absolutism, but rather contrasted relativism and fundamentalism, defining fundamentalism as the belief that ideals must be grounded in something already real, and relativism as denying that claim, was that I agree that there is no difference between the pope and philosophers like myself when it comes to the strength of our political convictions. If you want to put it that way, you can say we both believe in absolutes. The pope believes in different absolutes than philosophers like me. So I want to grant the point that everyone with moral convictions is as absolutistic as everybody else. But I want to say that that is not the issue that philosophers are discussing. They are discussing the question whether we need metaphysics, whether we need theology, whether we need a picture of the world as already holding the ideals that we wish to bring into existence.

About democracy as the notion is used in the United States: people like Dewey, defenders of social democracy like Dewey, would say, I think, that democracy is not itself an absolute. It is simply the best means to the greatest human happiness that we have been able to imagine so far. In the past we had other visions of what would maximize human happiness. Today our vision is of democracy. Tomorrow it may be of some other way of maximizing human happiness. But human happiness remains the only absolute in the area. We don't know now what the ideal society would look like. We don't even know whether it would be a democratic society, just as a thousand years ago we didn't know what the ideal society would look like, though we all thought it would be a Christian and Catholic society. It may turn out not to be a Christian and Catholic society. Perhaps it won't even turn out to be a democratic society. But if human beings can freely discuss how to make each other happier, it will still be an ideal society.

A MEMBER OF THE AUDIENCE   Don't you find it difficult to accept *sic et simpliciter* that one's desire is more or less licit in every case, as long as it is consonant with that of others? Don't you think that the massification of desires is acceptable only within the Christian framework of "love your neighbor as yourself"?

RICHARD RORTY   I think that the idea of a society in which everyone loves everyone else equally, or as they love themselves, is an impossible ideal. The ideal of a society in which everyone has enough respect for other people not to presume that one of their desires is intrinsically evil is a possible ideal. And it is the latter ideal that, through the growth of social democracy and tolerance, we have been gradually achieving in the last two centuries.

A MEMBER OF THE AUDIENCE   It is clear that the problem lies precisely in the three-way relation between relativism, absolutism, and fundamentalism. The objectionable form of relativism is not the claim that each single truth is relative to the setting in which it is expressed; that is quite right. But for me it is axiomatic that truth has meaning only if it is total, universal, and complete. No truth is meaningful if it is only particular and relative. So relative truth is subservient to total truth.

If we transfer this idea from the realm of theory to that of ethics, clearly the only thing deserving attack and condemnation is the attitude of those who want only their own individual happiness, or that of their own group, and exclude the happiness of others. So the best thing is to wish for the happiness of all. But is it possible to combine the maximum of happiness for ourselves with the happiness of all? This is certainly impossible. It is clearly something that could only be realized in a transcendental dimension. Naturally in this world we have to manage things so that the two things coexist somehow, therefore we can't exclude the homosexuals, we can't exclude women, we can't exclude the poor: they all deserve consideration.

But take the possibility that humankind might be destroyed if the happiness of only a small number is safeguarded. I could give examples. In that case, clearly we have to privilege the kind of choice that safeguards the survival of humanity. Because you can't be happy if you are dead, if your existence has been terminated. So the problem is complex from the point of view of the reality of this world. The solution that fuses both aspects—the maximum happiness of each and the totality of the happiness of all, of the truth of all—cannot be of this world. We can conceive it only in another dimension, a transcendental dimension.

RICHARD RORTY It seems to me that the notion of a universal truth and of a transcendent dimension are both expressions of the hope that there is something large and powerful on our side. Something large and powerful working on our behalf. Something in reality which is sympathetic to our goals. Religion is the traditional expression of that belief. As secularist politics gradually replaced theocratic politics in the West, it became more and more possible to substitute hope that there was something powerful on our side with simple hope that human beings would do certain things, that they could freely cooperate in certain ways. I think of the philosophy common to Mill, Dewey, and Habermas as saying: Now that we have made politics secular, let us also make politics non-metaphysical. Let us give up even secular ways of trying to assure ourselves that there is something large and powerful on our side. Let us try to make progress simply through hope for cooperation with one another, rather than in hope of achieving universal truth or contact with the transcendent.

GIANNI VATTIMO   Someone from the audience is asserting that the one does not exclude the other. But there is a problem. What about those who were burned at the stake? What if, in order to fulfill this notion of a totality of happiness, we have to burn heretics, old women, and so on? These things happened.

   The idea that God is a hope rather than an object, is one that even Dietrich Bonhoeffer shared, I believe. Because Bonhoeffer would have shied at the claim that "God exists." "There is" God? Where? Is he a knowable object? Think about that and you might start to see some merit in Rorty's position.

A MEMBER OF THE AUDIENCE   Professor Rorty, would a return from Catholicism, Islam, and Judaism back to that archetype of laicity, Odysseus, be possible and desirable in your view? Odysseus, endowed not with contemplative intelligence, *nous*, but with operational intelligence, *metis*, took on problems and solved them, *ut Deus non esset* [without reference to God]. Could we return to a laicity of that kind? It was already there in the ancient world.

RICHARD RORTY   I don't think that we can go back at all, either to the secularism of Odysseus or to the days of Mohammed or to the days of Christ or the days of Abraham. We know much more than any of these prophets and heroes and visionaries knew. We have accumulated more experience than they had. We are not closer to any universal truth than they are. We are not closer to anything transcendent than they were. We are simply more experienced, more able to see what will cause harm and what might do good. So I don't think that it's a question of returning, it's a question of constantly attempting to make the future still more different from the past.

A MEMBER OF THE AUDIENCE   Two short fables by way of objection. The first: I land on an island where the population likes to eat people who have never eaten other people, so they want to eat me, because I'm not a cannibal. They are a lot happier if they eat me, but I'm a lot less so. It's my individual happiness against that of an entire population. On what rational basis do I argue for my life? The second: imagine another island where the people love to make war. Happiness for them means overcoming others. Let's call it the island of Hobbes and Freud. Inclusion in that society means participation in the war of all against all. How do we envision happiness there? Is promoting individual happiness the right way to bring progress to that society? Hobbes would beg to differ.

RICHARD RORTY   I think that the question "On what basis can we show that they shouldn't eat us?" or "On what basis can we show that they shouldn't be brutal to us?" is an expression of the Platonic conviction that deep in the heart of every human being there is a fixed moral reference point, regardless of the way those human beings were raised, regardless of their culture, regardless of their tradition. I think we have no reason to believe that. So I think that once we give up the belief that simply by being human we know something to which appeal can be made, once we give up that idea, then we will be content no longer to be fundamentalists. We will agree that we have no way to convince people on these islands not to do what they have been trained to do, what they traditionally do. There is nothing in their human nature to appeal to, because humans don't have a nature. There is no structure of human existence. There are simply various ways in which human beings have come together in societies and have established traditions. Some of those traditions have made human beings much happier, some of them have made them much more miserable.

A MEMBER OF THE AUDIENCE   Yesterday there was a lecture by a French philosopher, the atheist Michel Onfray. What he said in short was: God does not exist, and Jesus is his son. Professor Onfray finds happiness only in stating this proposition. Could I have your comment on his stance? One more point: there is an American expression I heard recently that seems to me relevant to your lecture today: if you aren't looking for trouble, trouble will come looking for you. I would like to have your comment on these two subjects, if possible.

RICHARD RORTY   I'm not sure I have anything to say about the second. About the first, it seems to me that there have been many attempts by Christian thinkers to distinguish between the Old Testament religion of power and the New Testament religion of love, and to say that the history of Christianity is the gradual subsumption of power under love, or the gradual replacement of power as the chief attribute of the divine with love as the chief attribute of the divine. Gianni Vattimo's book *Credere di Credere* [to believe that one believes] seems to me one of the best recent expressions, at least among those I've read, of this attempt to rethink the Christian message. In Vattimo's book, the question of whether God has power over us no longer arises, because Vattimo interprets the Christian doctrine of the incarnation as God handing over all his power to man, the Father handing over all his power to the Son. This seems to me a very sympathetic reading of Christianity.

A MEMBER OF THE AUDIENCE You explain to us that neither reason nor experience helps us to choose between a transcendental and an immanentist perspective. Does that mean that we just have to resign ourselves to the fact that in this world everyone sticks to their own superstition, or is there a point at which we take stock, and we say: "No, it is preferable to pursue this course rather than the others"? That moment of stock-taking, of assessing the facts, isn't that democracy in action?

RICHARD RORTY I think yes, that is the application. Of course reading history and reading philosophy has an influence on which of the great visions of the world you will ally yourself with. But in the end I think we should give up the idea that either philosophy or history provides a neutral court of appeal to decide between us and our friends who are attracted by the alternative vision. We are gradually working out a form of social life in which atheists and Christians can live together in the same political arena. Three hundred years ago this would have been thought impossible. But we achieved it. It was a great imaginative project and it turned out to be a successful project. I hope we can hold on to this project and that it will become a model for the future course of moral progress.

GIANNI VATTIMO I have the impression that, as the last question shows, the idea is widespread in the general public that in the end everyone just sticks with their own convictions. But there is a whole middle ground between total, definitive truth, on the one hand, and "everything goes," on the other, and experience and history can supply us with what you might call rhetorical arguments *ad homines*. If someone says "I prefer the Beatles (or something even worse than the Beatles) to Beethoven," what can I do? All I can do is try to convince him: "Listen to this with me, hear how banal that chord is," and so on. More I cannot do. In history and experience I find not so much definitive arguments as rhetorical arguments. I don't know whether Richard Rorty agrees.

RICHARD RORTY   Yes. I don't mean to say that historical experience, reading history, reading literature, reading philosophy, talking with your friends, taking part in politics, is useless, that it's just a matter of arbitrary preference. All I want to say is that—I agree with you—we should stop opposing universal necessary truth and arbitrary preference, and say that no important decisions are made by an exercise of arbitrary preference, no important decisions are made by assured grounding in universal truth. We are all always somewhere in between.

PHILOSOPHY, RELIGION, AND RELIGIOUS BELIEF AFTER RORTY

G. ELIJAH DANN

A few years ago, I wrote *After Rorty: The Possibilities for Ethics and Religious Belief* in which I tried to outline, among other things, what ethics, the philosophy of religion, and religious belief might look like in light of Richard Rorty's metaphilosophical views.[1] The timing of this exploration was fortunate, as a couple months before my manuscript was due the very capable Santiago Zabala published a book based on a discussion of these topics that Rorty had with Gianni Vattimo.[2] Their conversation provided me with more theoretical fodder for my own study. Now, a few years later, I'd like to try to stoke the small flame a bit more to see if a little more light can be generated, especially in relation to this presentation and exchange by Richard Rorty and Gianni Vattimo.

Jeffrey Robbins's introduction has already explained Rorty's philosophical transition, but I'd like to add to it. In *After Rorty*, I offered what I thought was an apt, albeit hypothetical, analogy between Rorty having doubts about the philosophical tradition and a story (the hypothetical part) about Pope Benedict XVI. Imagine, I wrote, if the then Cardinal Joseph Ratzinger, while in the Papal Conclave after the death of Pope John Paul II, had awoken after the first day of the Conclave's meeting and, for a reason not particularly determinable, thought that he could no longer believe in God.

It's one thing, say, for the new atheists, like Richard Dawkins, Christopher Hitchens, Sam Harris and Daniel Dennett, to castigate and criticize religious belief. None had much involvement in organized religion. (And, dare I say, none has profound understanding of Christian theology, or, even in general, the phenomenon of religion.)[3] In any case, it's quite another thing for those who are steeped and trained in a given tradition, and who are its highly articulate advocates, to have a change of mind on the value of a tradition, then upping the ante by becoming vocal detractors of the very tradition they once embraced. In the case of the Church, it can ignore, even tolerate a Dawkins, Hitchens, Harris, or Dennett. Yet the Church will feel a sharp chill down its spine when those who have been its greatest defenders turn their backs on it. This reaction isn't unique to established religious groups. It also holds for other established organizations and institutions, even one—like the philosophical community—that extols the virtue of critical, unbiased, and clearheaded thinking.

Of course, Cardinal Ratzinger, now Pope Benedict XVI, had no change of heart. But in midcareer, Richard Rorty did have one about the various tasks of traditional philosophy. His eventual abdication generated a particular sort of resentment from the philosophical community—a typical reaction to the renunciation of one of its leading advocates. It would've been no different in the halls of seminaries if Cardinal Ratzinger had thought the gig was up for religious belief and Catholicism. Ordinarily, this sort of doubt would go unnoticed by the wider philosophical community. In Rorty's case however, trained at Chicago and then Yale by some of the most notable philosophers of the twentieth century—Rudolph Carnap, Charles Hartshorne, Richard McKeon, and Paul Weiss—he showed himself to be a sharply skilled philosopher who delved deeply into the traditional inquiries with impressive acumen. Then, while teaching at Princeton in the 1960s, because of his colleagues' predilections toward analytic philosophy, he took time to understand this prominent philosophical school of thought.[4] By then, it could've easily have been assumed that Rorty would one day command the attention of the philosophical community by doing cutting-edge philosophical analysis.

The analysis indeed came about, but not in the way it was expected.[5] Rorty began to chart his doubts about the philosophical tradition in *Philosophy and the Mirror of Nature*, published in 1979. When it appeared, it was interpreted by some as an attempt to pull apart the very tradition that Rorty had so diligently studied. In relatively quick succession his other volumes appeared, expanding his metaphilosophical critique: *Consequences of Pragmatism* (1982), *Contingency, Irony, and Solidarity* (1989), *Objectivity, Relativism, and Truth* (1991), *Essays on Heidegger and Others* (1991), and *Truth and Progress* (1998).

Throughout these volumes Rorty challenges squarely the core inquiries of "first philosophy"—or, Philosophy.[6] One of his key targets throughout these volumes is realism, with its representational theory of knowledge. "Realist philosophers say the only true source of evidence is the world as it is in itself."[7] So the mind's task is to take the empirical input—"the given"—and for the generated thoughts to then represent, or "mirror the reality," of the exterior world. In turn, this exercise of the mind's mirroring the world by representation becomes a "'rational reconstruction' of our knowledge."[8] By means of this representation, if done rightly, we will have then established a correspondence with the world, deriving truth.[9]

The other feature of traditional philosophy that Rorty takes to task is foundationalism—the notion that there is an ultimate resting place that is the ground, or "foundation" for our most basic beliefs:

> [It is] an epistemological view which can be adopted by those who suspend judgment on the realist's claim that reality has an intrinsic nature. A foundationalist need only claim that every belief occupies a place in a natural, transcultural, transhistorical order of reasons—an order which eventually leads the inquirer back to one or another "ultimate source of evidence".[10]

Accompanying a very close examination of the central projects of first philosophy throughout these volumes, he also works through and presents concomitant redefinitions of the nomenclature held to be of greatest interest to the traditional philosopher. Rorty's criticism traverses the spectrum of philosophy, from the efforts of analytic philosophy (such as studies in the philosophy of language, epistemology, and metaphysics) clear over to the so-called Continental side. Although the process of philosophizing is different for Continental philosophers, whether powered by phenomenology, existentialism, or deconstructionism, there is also a conviction for them, just like many of the philosophers working in analytic philosophy, that there is the "really real" to be uncovered.[11] This is what philosophy has become, holding the age-old conviction that once the technique of its algorithm is applied, then Knowledge, Reality, and Truth will be obtained.

The perennial problems of philosophy had their beginnings with Plato, who expounded on the notion that there is something beyond the natural, corporeal, and temporal world (the realm of "shadows") that must be contemplated in order for us to achieve enlightenment and, as a result, upon death, emancipation from this fleshly existence.

The philosopher's task, Plato believed, was to recollect the eternal realm of the Forms, the realm where Truth, Beauty, and Goodness reside in their perfection. This realm is where the Forms of all earthly representations exist in perfect harmony, from the muck and sludge of the earthworm to the magnificent scenes of nature like a mountaintop and, more abstractly, the deeply complex algorithm lurking in the mind of the mathematician. Only by contemplating these Forms will we be able to know the True Nature of Reality, including Moral Reality, and armed with such knowledge we will be able to intelligibly understand our corporeal world, and, by consequence, ultimately escape it upon death.

As Rorty saw it, two thousand years later, the philosophical tradition with its assorted investigations and tasks put into gear by Plato hasn't paid off. Philosophers, taking up the challenge by Plato to define and distinguish the inevitable dualisms of Knowledge vs. Opinion, Reality vs. Shadows, Truth vs. Error, produced a multitude of distinctions, wandered down innumerable labyrinths, carried through various investigations, but always bringing more questions and more problems, all seemingly without end. Today, few philosophers hold to Plato's more ephemeral views, like the contemplation of the Forms. There is, however, a remaining allegiance to his original ambitions:

> [They] think of their discipline as one which discusses perennial, eternal problems—problems which arise as soon as one reflects. Some of these concern the difference between human beings and other beings, and are crystallized in questions concerning the relation between the mind and the body. Other problems concern the legitimization of claims to know, and are crystallized in questions concerning the "foundations of knowledge."[12]

Taken further:

> [This is] the original Platonic strategy of postulating novel *objects* for treasured propositions to correspond to, and the Kantian strategy of finding *principles* which are definatory of the essence of knowledge, or representation, or morality, or rationality. But this difference is unimportant compared to the common urge to escape the vocabulary and practices of one's own time and find something ahistorical and necessary to cling to.[13]

This "urge to escape" is what Rorty and a long succession of intellectuals have pointed out (to borrow from Nietzsche), as the rather *human, all too human*, political, mundane, emotional, psychological elements—but altogether powerful ones—that go into the promoting of a given belief, tradition, or school of thought.

Alongside Rorty's more critical volumes on traditional philosophy, where he worked through the reasons he thought professional philosophy and its vocabulary had to change direction, he also published works such as *Truth, Politics, and 'Post-Modernism'* (1997), *Achieving Our Country* (1998), and *Philosophy and Social Hope* (1999) where he tried to show what this overall transformation might look like. By the time *Philosophy as Cultural Politics* (2007) appeared, instead of the further pulling apart the obsession "with the primal world of some final vocabulary, with truth or objectivity,"[14] Rorty's attention had turned clearly to the pressing issues of contemporary society: gender, race, and class discrimination, to name a few. His admitted dependence was on John Dewey, who emphasized that we should turn our intellectual energy to addressing the "problems of society," envisioned as "clarifying the ideas men and women have on those issues that divide them."[15]

Jeffrey Robbins and Gianni Vattimo have already reviewed the manner in which Rorty criticized the philosophical tradition and its key terms. In the remaining pages, I want to describe and expand Rorty's view of religious belief. But to make the description as clear as possible, without being too repetitive, some of his key redefinitions of traditional philosophical terminology should be kept in mind.

Rationality, a fundamental term in first philosophy, is not some quality of thinking unique to the philosophical mind, one based on a reflection and concise understanding of the terminology, distinctions, and qualifications in the philosophical tradition, honed as a graduate student and then fully bestowed after successfully defending the Ph.D. thesis. Instead, as Rorty sees it, *to be rational* names a set of moral virtues:

> Tolerance, respect for the opinions of those around one, willingness to listen, reliance on persuasion rather than force. These are the virtues which members of a civilized society must possess if the society is to endure. In this sense of "rational," the word means something more like "civilized" than like "methodological." When so construed, the distinction between the rational and the irrational has nothing in particular to do with the difference between the arts and the sciences. On this construction, to be rational is simply to discuss any topic—religious, literary, or scientific—in a way which eschews dogmatism, defensiveness, and righteous indignation.[16]

This isn't to say that philosophy hasn't been productive over the centuries in charting out some of the terminologies, distinctions, and qualifications that have contributed to the avoidance of dogmatism and the cultivating of this "tolerance." Consider Socratic dialogue, where we carefully reflect on the terms and claims we make and whether they are coherent, consistent, or contradictory; Aristotle's description of ethical virtue; Hobbes's observation that living in the state of nature would be "solitary, poor, nasty, brutish and short" and that we need a social contract to avert such an end; Kant's emphasis on not being free-riders regarding our moral behavior; Sartre's "existence precedes essence"; and Rawls's "veil of ignorance" in matters of justice.[17] These are only a few examples from the history of philosophy that evidence Rorty's virtues. These virtues hold, however, not because they somehow mirror reality (including moral reality), are foundational to our reasoning, or capture the essence of Truthfulness. Instead, borrowing from William James, we think that, "'true' resembles 'good' or 'rational' in being a normative notion, a compliment paid to sentences that seem to be paying their way and that fit in with other sentences which are doing so."[18]

To keep our beliefs stable, is it enough that the terms we choose to use "pay their way" and "fit in with the other sentences"? There is more to Rorty's conception of how we should think about our language. His pragmatist understanding is summed up in Dewey:

> If ideas, meanings, conceptions, notions, theories, systems are instrumental to an active reorganization of the given environment, to a removal of some specific trouble and perplexity, then the test of their validity and value lies in accomplishing this work. If they succeed in their office, they are reliable, sound, valid, good, true. If they fail to clear up confusion to eliminate defects, if they increase confusion, uncertainty, and evil when they are acted upon, then they are false.[19]

When we turn our attention to how Rorty's metaphilosophy can transform religious belief, it'll be important to keep in mind the pragmatist redefinition of how we determine what is "reliable, sound, valid, good, [and] true." We can anticipate some further implications for this transformation in another passage from Rorty:

> If there are no privileged representations in this mirror, then it will no longer answer to the need for a touchstone for choice between justified and unjustified claims upon our belief. Unless some other such framework can be found, the abandonment of the image of the Mirror leads us to abandon the notion of philosophy as a discipline which adjudicates the claims of science and religion, mathematics and poetry, reason and sentiment, allocating an appropriate place to each.[20]

While there is value learning about the philosophical tradition, its efforts, inquiries, and missteps, we should put to rest the Grand Investigation of perennial philosophy. Instead, our intellectual efforts need redirection and should be aimed toward addressing the most pressing issues of contemporary society.[21] As Vattimo commented in his introduction:

> So Rorty's stance imposed a different horizon on the problem of observational truth: no longer that of inspecting how things are but that of operating in (and on) reality. Pragmatism doesn't mean just "what is true is what works" but also "we are in the world not to inspect how things are, but to produce, to make, to transform reality." Toward what end? Toward our happiness. Are we meant to feel happy when we have ascertained how things are? Why would we? If someone is ill and is told that she is ill because she has a wasting disease, will she feel happy? No, unless you also give her the drug that will cure her. In that circumstance, knowing the truth serves a purpose, the purpose of trying not to be too unhappy.

Rorty's remarks, along with Vattimo's, approach Habermas's sense of "communicative rationality." This is when "our obligation to be rational is exhausted by our obligation to take account of other people's doubts and objections to our beliefs."[22]

Rorty and the Philosophy of Religion

In *After Rorty*, my central aim was to show the significance his thought had for religion (as a scholarly discipline) and religious belief (as a private pursuit), after the "demise" of the philosophical tradition. My intent was not, as some evangelical philosophers and theologians are wont to do with notable intellectuals or public figures, to Christianize him. Nor was it to demonstrate that the most current (or fashionable) thinking in secular, scholarly thinking—a group that Rorty clearly belongs to—lends itself to Christian belief, or at least to theism. These are, among other things, all strategies for proselytizing,[23] and quite outside my range of interests.

Although I was raised in a conservative Christian environment and went on to graduate studies in theology in the 1980s, I soon stepped out of mainstream Christianity and turned my academic interests to philosophy. While I returned to study theology a decade later, it was under the direction of a "death of God" theologian. By that time, in contrast to what Rorty (borrowing from Max Weber) calls being "religiously unmusical,"[24] I was, in fact, religiously musical, though I was wholly unenthusiastic about organized religion, especially when it came to how ecclesiastical bodies approached social issues like the so-called hot-button topics of religious conservatives: abortion, embryonic stem-cell research, physician-assisted suicide, and same-sex marriage, to name the most popular.

While I was highly critical about the way organized religion be-haved in the public square on these matters, I knew this behavior wasn't the totality of religion or religious belief. Perhaps what helped me most in this conviction began with recognizing how traditional theology was as susceptible to Rorty's doubts as perennial philosophy.

The historical relationship between philosophy and theology, with their compatible interests on matters of metaphysics and epistemol-ogy, isn't very difficult to demonstrate. Martin Heidegger wrote that "Western metaphysics . . . since its beginning with the Greeks has em-inently been both ontology and theology."[25] Expanding this descrip-tion Dewey wrote:

> Through a variety of channels, especially Neo-Platonism and St. Au-gustine, these ideas found their way into Christian theology; and great scholastic thinkers taught that the end of man is to know True Being, that knowledge is completive, that True Being is pure Immaterial Mind, and to know it is Bliss and Salvation. While this knowledge can-not be achieved in this stage of life nor without supernatural aid, yet so far as it is accomplished it assimilates the human mind to the divine essence and so constitutes salvation. Through this taking over of the conception of knowledge as Contemplative into the dominant religion of Europe, multitudes were affected who were totally innocent of the-oretical philosophy.[26]

Heidegger, and to a lesser extent Dewey, are regarded as suspect commentators by many conventional philosophers, but even the staid Thomist philosopher Etienne Gilson, never accused of schol-arly hyperbole, understood that "Christian philosophy arose at the juncture of Greek philosophy and of the Jewish-Christian reli-gious revelation, Greek philosophy providing the technique for a

rational explanation of the world, and the Jewish-Christian revelation providing religious beliefs of incalculable philosophical im-
port."[27] Habermas describes this relationship as "mutual compenetration": "The mutual compenetration of Christianity and Greek
metaphysics not only produced the intellectual form of theological
dogmatics and a hellenization of Christianity (which was not in every
sense a blessing). It also promoted the assimilation by philosophy of
genuinely Christian ideas."[28]

Despite the historical, symbiotic relationship between philosophy
and theology, I still thought that accepting Rorty's metaphilosophical critique should not bring us to think that religion is unavoidably
malignant and that we should put an end to all forms of religious
belief. Nonetheless, managing it becomes a devil's bargain for some
believers.

The Division Between the Private and the Public

On the one hand, philosophy, with its conceptual tools of analysis,
has no privileged, epistemological vantage point from which it can
describe and adjudicate *reality*. This philosophical vista has been described metaphorically as the "God's-eye standpoint," the aspiration
to have "somehow broken out of our language and our beliefs and
tested them against something known without their aid."[29] Without
such a vantage point, philosophers, like everyone else, can't make
heavy-handed criticisms about religious belief on the basis that it
isn't "rational," doesn't correspond with reality, or because there is
no objective referent for the term "God." Instead, "rationality," "reality," and "objectivity" have been redefined as "reasonability" in an attempt to extend intersubjective agreement as far as possible.[30] Under
this redescription, "knowledge," like "truth," becomes a simple

"compliment paid to the beliefs which we think so well justified that, for the moment, further justification is not needed."[31] Applied to God talk, it is "never an objection to a religious belief that there is no evidence for it,"[32] and so, at best, the religiously unmusical can only have an agnostic or skeptical view about religious belief and the existence of God. After the demise of the philosophical tradition, this implication has escaped the notice of hardcore philosophical atheists as well as their budding companions, today's new atheists.[33]

On the other hand, because of Rorty's critique, the same conceptual restraints placed on philosophical atheism hold also for philosophical theology and its own talk about Truth, objectivity, and metaphysics, all put to use in its traditional, heavy-handed claims about religious knowledge (e.g., that the existence and nature of God can somehow be demonstrated and explained). The restraints also spill over to the rest of the typical esoteric dialect of contemporary popular Christian culture that, especially in the public square, appeals to God and scripture for deriving its moral dictates uses religious experience as the basis for accepting the truthfulness of the Christian religion.[34] In short, the devil's bargain is that the same constraints that hold for criticizing religious belief also apply to those with religious belief:

> President Bush made a good point when he said, in a speech designed to please Christian fundamentalists, that "atheism is a faith" because it is "subject to neither confirmation nor refutation by means of argument or evidence." But the same goes, of course, for theism. Neither those who affirm nor those who deny the existence of God can plausibly claim that they have evidence for their views. Being religious, in the modern West, does not have much to do with the explanation of specific observable phenomenon.[35]

If there are going to be formal debates over the existence of God, neither atheists nor theists will have the theoretical, conceptual ammunition to raise against their opponent to demonstrate God's non-existence or existence. Yet it doesn't follow that all topics related to religion and religious belief will be scratched out. At least in his later writings, Rorty's target wasn't so much the private religious beliefs of the average person but rather the ecclesiastical authorities who claim to speak for God then seek to impose dictates on secular society in the public square. For Rorty, the problem is organized religion. Its theological language, woven from the same Platonic assumptions as traditional philosophy, shares a conceptual framework about the True and the Good. Organized religion then wades into public matters with its economic, political, and cultural clout to tell us the way things have to be epistemically and metaphysically and, with the goods gained from inquiry into those disciplines, what is morally required from us.

There are a number of examples of how this line of thinking works, but as in his lecture printed in this book, his particular focus was the established church's opposition to homosexuality. The church's stance draws from typical metaphysical assumptions: that God exists; that he has revealed himself in scripture; that he has set out moral dictates; and that society has the obligation to heed his prescripts.[36] As a consequence, if, in the public square, we decide to debate the topic of same-sex marriage, the Catholic Church's position will be that it is a practice condemned by God and that scripture declares it an "abomination." Rorty, quoting approvingly from one of his critics, describes this manner of discourse as a "conversation-stopper": "One good way to end a conversation—or to start an argument—is to tell a group of well-educated professionals that you hold a political position (preferably a controversial one, such as being against abortion or pornography) because it is required by our understanding of God's will."[37]

The Catholic Church's position is a conversation-stopper largely because the metaphysical assumptions built into its moral stance—that God exists and the Bible is authoritative on moral matters—renders its normative view opaque and, as such, unsuitable for public dialectic. In his dialogue with the Catholic Church, Habermas also raises the issue of the need for transparent language in the public square:

> [A] philosophy that is aware of its fallibility and of its fragile position within the differentiated structures of modern society will insist on the generic distinction (which is not at all meant in a pejorative sense) between the secular discourse that claims to be accessible to all men and the religious discourse that is dependent upon the truths of revelation.[38]

I think it would be safe to say that Rorty would agree with Habermas here (although Rorty, as we'll see, wants to change the dependency that religious discourse has on metaphysics). But specifically on the point of how obligation is carried out in the public square, Rorty cites approvingly from James's utilitarian view on the subject: "The obligation to justify one's beliefs arises only when one's habits of action interfere with the fulfillment of others' needs." Or, said otherwise, the justification is necessary to "the extent to which the actions of religious believers frustrate the needs of other human beings."[39]

These passages set up Rorty's division between public and private pursuits. If people decide to have religious beliefs, then they need to be privatized. The cleavage between the public and private, according to Rorty, can be found with Jefferson and the Enlightenment compromise: by privatizing religious beliefs, there is the guarantee for religious liberty in exchange.[40] "On our view," Rorty noted, "religion is unobjectionable as long as it is privatized—as long as ecclesiastical institutions do not attempt to rally the faithful behind political proposals and as long as believers and unbelievers agree to follow a policy of live and let live."[41] Rorty points out that the private/public distinction doesn't trivialize religious pursuits as there are many types of private pursuits of perfection, some lighthearted and some quite serious. As privatized pursuits, they are in the domain of one's own personal interest, for reasons of one's own preference, and are not the business of anyone else.

Being told that religious beliefs must be privatized and left out of the political sphere is something many believers find grossly inconsistent, even hypocritical. Rorty's detractors, such as those mentioned above by Robbins, have asked how talk about the will of God is different from "the will of any of the brilliant philosophers of the liberal tradition, or, for that matter, the will of the Supreme Court of the United States."[42]

Liberal theory, however, doesn't have to demonstrate the difference. It only has to show that moral decisions on matters of public policy in a pluralist and democratic state are satisfied, or justified, by a particular political test: the "ability to gain assent from people who retain radically diverse ideas about the point and meaning of human life, about the path to private perfection."[43] Appeals to the will of God through quoting the Bible, church doctrine, and ecclesiastical authorities, fail this test for public values because it isn't clear how these appeals can be adjudicated.

In a conversation Rorty had in 2005, he gave an example from philosophical metaphysics that is analogous to arguments over religious values. The main problem with metaphysics, he said, is that "it is a game without rules." For example, if it is claimed that, "'the nature of reality is spiritual,' as the heirs of German absolute idealists said in the 19th century, and somebody else says, 'No, the nature of reality is to be made up of atoms and void': how is anybody able to decide a question like that? . . . The trouble with metaphysics is that anyone can say anything and get away with it."[44] Similarly, when someone says that the will of God needs to be followed when it comes to the placement of the Ten Commandments in public schools, it isn't at all clear how such a claim can be adjudicated. (Of course, religious values are not monolithic, even within a particular religion, so there also remains the problem of how to decide between competing religious values. For example, Roman Catholicism teaches that birth control is a mortal sin, a view the Protestant churches do not hold. As a public-policy debate—whether birth control should be available to everyone—how would we go about deciding this moral matter?)

This strikes at the heart of Jeffrey Stout's major criticism, that Rorty thinks religious believers have no right to voice their values in the public square. Rorty doesn't say this. Instead, he maintains that, like everyone else, religious believers must subject their values to the political test. If they cannot do so, their right to continue voicing their views remains, but the rest of us have no obligation to listen to them.[45] Habermas's caution to this obligation, that the "liberal state must not transform the requisite institutional separation of religion and politics into an undue mental or psychological burden for those of its citizens who follow a faith,"[46] belies the sentiment that religious believers think that their "moral convictions are more deeply interwoven with their self-identity than those of atheists with theirs. They seem unwilling to admit that the role of Enlightenment ideology in giving meaning to the lives of atheists is just as great as Christianity's role in giving meaning to [their own lives]."[47]

In light of current culture wars between the new atheists and Christian conservatives, Rorty's estimation of religious belief clearly wouldn't find favor with members of organized religion. However, the new atheists would be equally unimpressed with Rorty's view as they think that religious belief—in whatever form it might take, even if it is privatized—is a "delusion," that it "poisons everything," that atheists are "Brights," and that religious faith, in all its forms, should end.[48] For his part, despite Rorty's extensive criticism of ecclesiastical institutions and their mucking about in the public square, I doubt that he would have sided with the new atheists, and not just for the reason Robbins gives in his foreword, that they erect inadvertently "a double or surrogate for God on the basis of a philosophical foundationalism." Rorty would have also disagreed with them because, while he had little difficulty with a philosophical or cultural fidelity to atheism, he had the worldly sophistication to understand that evil comes in many forms. Even if religious belief did not exist in our world, corruption, deviousness, xenophobia, racism, and sexism still would.[49]

Nevertheless, because religious belief, even the public sort, will certainly continue into the future, Rorty thought that there had to be a mutual restraint between nonbelievers and believers: "People who find themselves quite unable to take an interest in the question of whether God exists have no right to be contemptuous of people who believe passionately in his existence or of people who deny it with equal passion." Here's the corresponding obligation for those with religious belief: "Nor do either of the latter have a right to be contemptuous of those to whom the dispute seems pointless."[50] If both the new atheists and conservative Christians respected these restraints—with the new atheists toning down the rhetoric and the religious right keeping to privatized religious belief—the so-called American culture wars could find a basis for a treaty.

This treaty is unlikely to happen anytime soon between those who are highly critical of all forms of religious belief and those who wish it to have a high, public visibility. Nevertheless, if we take Rorty's post-philosophical position seriously, where no one enjoys a God's-eye vantage point over culture, morality, and human affairs, a third way opens for those who wish to pursue their religious interests. It is a bearing that Rorty himself began to explore near the end of his life.

In Dialogue with the Religiously Musical

Up to his death Richard Rorty remained, as he put it, religiously unmusical, choosing to further describe himself as "anticlerical" instead of an "atheist." "Anticlericalism is a political view, not an epistemological or metaphysical one. It is the view that ecclesiastical institutions, despite all the good they do—despite all the comfort they provide to those in need or in despair—are dangerous to the health of democratic societies."[51] Consistent with his enduring personality, however, Rorty was always disposed to engaging in dialogue with others. Most certainly owing to his broad intellectual interests, he was also able to avoid the reductionist view of religion proffered by today's new atheists—that the behavior of religious institutions is the sum of religion and that once you've shown the corruption of these institutions you will have demonstrated that religion is a delusion.

While the practice of religion by these institutions certainly deserves this criticism—something that Rorty also offered readily—religion could be described, even practiced differently. To this end, Rorty offered rather extensive descriptions for how religion could be a private pursuit of perfection after the demise of the tradition.

A Pragmatic Philosophy of Religion

Rorty's pragmatism gave life to the philosophically minded by directing their intellectual efforts toward addressing the problems of society. Similarly, religious thought and behavior can as well be practiced pragmatically. In an article entitled "Religious Faith, Intellectual Responsibility, and Romance,"[52] borrowing from John Stuart Mill, Charles Saunders Peirce, and William James, Rorty weaves the main pillars of his metaphilosophy into a pragmatic description of religious faith, summarized in the following terms:

1   Placing aside talk about Truth and Reason, our only responsibility, philosophically and morally, is to our fellow human beings, not some "sublime dimension of being" or "the starry heavens."[53]
2   This responsibility is "to make our beliefs cohere with one another, and to our fellow humans to make them cohere with one another."[54]
3   We examine our beliefs by how they are "habits of action," not on whether they represent the world.
4   What emerges is a utilitarian ethics of belief, which treats a belief as a habit of action.
5   Placed into the context of the philosophy of religion, a utilitarian philosophy of religion must "also treat being religious as a habit of action."[55]

The positive components of what it means to be "religious" is similar to a secular, pragmatic, Deweyan understanding of our moral obligation to address the problems of society. Consequently, religious practice—at least in part—owes its moral obligation to our "fellow humans" not by trying to mirror morality to scripture and doctrine or through appeals to arcane principles and beliefs. Coherence of belief, as habits of actions, is its guidepost.

In Dialogue with Gianni Vattimo—Further Possibilities

Within these pragmatic limits—habits of action, beliefs that co-here—Rorty gave further thought to how religion may be understood in one of his last recorded discussions on the topic with Gianni Vatti-mo and Santiago Zabala (*The Future of Religion*). Evidencing his prag-matic spirit, Rorty understood that there were admirable elements to religion, at least the nonclerical sort. This was a slight shift in Rorty's estimation of religion, in contrast to the more negative com-ments (or better, quips) sprinkled about in his earlier philosophical volumes.

Having been friends with Vattimo, Rorty became acquainted with another sense of religion, to the point that he conceded that "if you want something else, then a religion that has been taken out of the epistemic arena, a religion that finds the question of theism versus atheism uninteresting, may be just what suits your solitude."[56] I'm not sure where Rorty may have found this sense of religion in Vat-timo's writings, but there are plenty of options. Perhaps it was Vat-timo's earlier work, *Belief*, where he described "the dissolution of metaphysics," or *After Christianity*, where he continued to expand the implications for Christian belief without metaphysics.[57]

Wherever Rorty gleaned the possibility of this sense of religion, for him, its suitability is captured by Vattimo because he "puts aside the attempt to connect religion with truth and so has no use for notions such as 'symbolic' or 'emotional' or 'metaphorical' or 'moral' truth."[58] This provides a conceptual steppingstone in Vattimo's description of religion because it has "no internal dynamic, no inherent teleology to human history; there is no great drama to be unfolded, but only the hope that love may prevail."[59]

Where does this lead, theologically speaking? Rorty, sounding surprisingly pastoral, offers commentary on Vattimo's strategy:

> [It treats] the Incarnation as God's sacrifice of all his power and authority, as well as all his otherness. The Incarnation was an act of *kenosis*, the act in which God turned everything over to human beings. This enables Vattimo to make his most startling and most important claim: that "secularization . . . is the constitutive trait of authentic religious experience."[60]

Rorty is right to see the significance of Vattimo's description of kenosis. According to traditional theological Christology, it is literally an "emptying": specifically, that the Son of God became man, the Messiah, submitting himself to the will of his father. But Vattimo also sees in the Incarnation the end of metaphysics. God became man, piercing transcendence and immersing in immanence, removing the metaphysical between God and humanity.[61]

Once more, like a careful theologian expounding scripture, Rorty describes further this sense of "authentic religious experience":

> 1 Corinthians 13 is an equally useful text for both religious people like Vattimo, whose sense of what transcends our present condition is bound up with a feeling of dependence, and for nonreligious people like myself, for whom this sense consists simply in hope for a better human future. The difference between these two sorts of people is that between unjustifiable gratitude and unjustifiable hope. This is not a matter of conflicting beliefs about what really exists and what does not.[62]

In short, people with different private interests "can work together side by side on the basis of different ontological interpretations of something. . . . A nonmetaphysical religiousness is also a nonmissionary one."[63]

Nonmetaphysical Religiousness

This view of religion, with the metaphysics gone, will no doubt be seen by many as incoherent. For them, irrespective of the kenosis, religion cannot escape being a metaphysical project since, by definition, its themes deal with what is beyond the natural realm. In Vattimo's recent, largely autobiographical work, *Not Being God*, he describes again, this time abridged, how a nonmetaphysical religiousness is possible. This is a position that he now characterizes as "weak thought."[64]

Vattimo tells how, while in the mountains, he started reading Nietzsche. It was here that Vattimo discovered for himself an enduring "fundamental image": "modern man is wandering around in history as if it were a theme park or a storehouse of theatrical masks, trying on this one and that one."[65] The second part of Vattimo's "twofold turn," was reading Heidegger's *Letter on Humanism*, discovering that, "we are not on a plane where there is mankind alone, but on which there is above all and principally Being." But, "not only have we forgotten what Being means, we have forgotten that we have forgotten."[66] Vattimo explains:

The forgetting of Being was a difficulty that Heidegger was never able to resolve:

He oscillates between nostalgia and awareness that the whole history of philosophy in the West, metaphysics, is over and that it's a good thing it is. Time to move on. Because on one hand, Being is the most important thing there is; it's precisely what allows man to be, it's what illuminates reality. Yet at the same time Plato's Being, the Ideas existing in Hyperuranium, which then become the Cartesian cogito, the absolute truth, the Christian paradise, and so on down to scientific positivism, all these putatively objective truths are the negation of Being and so deserve merely to die.[67]

Vattimo then draws Nietzsche and Heidegger back together again, first with Nietzsche's implication that the "dissolution of the 'real' world" allows for humanity's liberation from being bound to "objective limits." This liberation from absolutes now brings us the responsibility to review and sort through our beliefs. Instead of values and principles imposed on us, "in order to bear this liberty we have to become overmen." This is the key to understanding Nietzsche's infamous pronouncement that "God is dead." It isn't a proclamation of atheism; it rather signifies "that there is no ultimate foundation" and that humanity must now step out of the shadows of metaphysics, and the variously imposed "theatrical masks" of transcendence of morality and meaning and begin to acquire its own sense of values, ethically and existentially.[68]

Heidegger, at least as Vattimo sees him, shares Nietzsche's "polemic against metaphysics," stipulated as "the whole European philosophical tradition from Parmenides on, that believes it can grasp an ultimate foundation of reality in the form of an objective structure located outside of time and history."[69] This is the structural conception of Being that Heidegger rejects.

Finally, "if we are bearers of hopes, feelings, fear, projects ... finite beings, with a past and a future, and not just appearances, then Being cannot be thought in terms of objectivistic metaphysics."[70] For those who choose to continue to speak about God, it must always be done in a *forgetful* manner—as if it isn't—or, at best, as if it might not be.

While Vattimo readily admits this isn't Heidegger's interpretation, the implication should nonetheless be that "the only possible history of Being is the growing lighter, the losing weight (*alleggerimento*) of Being itself. The history of Being is the history of how objective truth gradually dissolves; therefore it is nihilism." It is here where Vattimo brings Nietzsche back into the picture, as it is his "sketching" of nihilism that Vattimo wants to retain.[71]

In a few beautiful, poetic paragraphs, in keeping with Rorty's privatized sense of religion, Vattimo charts out the sense of this forgetfulness: "Being is confirmed as that which illuminates things without being identified with things." This is a "growing lighter" but also a "growing more distant." This history of Being, if there is one, "is a history of distancing, not of drawing closer. Being illuminates to the extent that it withdraws." If faith persists, it cannot have God as an object to be studied and venerated. As Vattimo reminds us, quoting Bonhoeffer, "A God who is, is not."[72]

Considering this original religious sentiment (which, by virtue of its subject matter, is a distanced history), with its acknowledged lightness (in the absence of doctrine), with no attempt to identify this feeling with a Being, the spirit of forgetfulness is retained. It walks a razor-sharp line by considering this particular sentiment, and if at some point we wish to use the word "God," it won't be to designate an object but "who is not." This was the beginning of God as *forgetfulness*, God without metaphysics.

This description from Vattimo is compatible with Rorty's metaphilosophy, and it's one that also resonates with a number of current thinkers and religious believers. For example, it is a thread of thought that the philosopher Robert Solomon also adopted before his sudden and untimely passing. In his remarkable book *Spirituality for the Skeptic*, Solomon writes, "Spirituality, I have come to see, is nothing less than the thoughtful love of life." His description would have been unproblematic for Rorty and Vattimo, as it is within the borders of how they, too, understand post-philosophical religious belief. It is "a nonreligious, noninstitutional, nontheological, nonscriptural, nonexclusive sense of spirituality, one which is not self-righteous, which is not based on Belief, which is not dogmatic, which is not antiscience, which is not other-worldly, which is not uncritical or cultist or kinky."[73] In short, it is a *"naturalized* spirituality."[74] Because it is privatized and doesn't seek for "other-worldly" Truth, it won't become mesmerized by its experience or by language or believing that there has to be transcendental pursuits, the very impetus for proselytizing. Truth, as Nietzsche realized, brings obligation—the obligation to impose one's belief on the world and to insist on this acceptance by everyone else.

In *The Future of Religion*, Rorty, Vattimo, and Zabala tried to give some sense about where things are headed, religiously speaking. Vattimo gave careful attention to this matter previously in *Belief* and *After Christianity*. In the latter, he has a particularly apt description of the effect the end of metaphysics has on belief in God and "the God of the Bible":

> Since God can no longer be upheld as an ultimate foundation, as the absolute metaphysical structure of the real, it is possible, once again, to believe in God. True, it is not the God of metaphysics or of medieval scholasticism. But that is not the God of the Bible, of the Book that was dissolved and dismissed by modern rationalist and absolutist metaphysics.[75]

I can't imagine a better way of putting my own sense of religious belief, stimulated by my imagination, considering the world and universe that surrounds me in all its splendor. Moreover, even though
interest in organized religion by others will continue, there are also
indications that people are looking for the sort of "spirituality" that
Rorty, Vattimo, and Solomon have described.

*Religion as a Private Pursuit After the Tradition—
Some Final Thoughts*

The writer of a recent article in the magazine *Philosophy Now* noted
the lamentations of the archbishop of Birmingham, who, in his own
book, *The Nation That Forgot God*, remarks that "faith has been rel-
egated to an individual pursuit, and the country has sought to define
itself by secular and material standards."[76] How we consider the archbishop's remarks depends on which side of the fence we are on.

Certainly there are many, like the archbishop, who wish to retain a
robust and very public sense of religion, religious belief, and theological doctrine. This is a stance held by various intellectuals, including
Christian philosophers, politicians, pastors, theologians, as well as
many laypeople.[77] But what the archbishop sees as regrettable would
be seen by many others as society's progression into political, religious, and moral autonomy.[78]

Rorty, in the latter group, while not going as far as the new atheists,
nevertheless has contributed to the critical analysis of religion and
religious belief. First, in the course of his voluminous writings, he set
out substantial reasons for his metaphilosophical position. Second,
because of theology's close historical and intellectual relationship
with traditional philosophy, Rorty's critique now has a clear effect
on religion, religious belief, and its discourse. In post-philosophical

society (and in contrast to the new atheists, who want to banish all forms of religion), religion remains, but only as a "privatized pursuit of perfection." The privatization is necessary because there is no epistemological vantage point, philosophical or theological, whereby grandiose proclamations about Reality can be made and then used to measure against the truthfulness of our other beliefs. Finally, while Rorty holds to a rigorous appraisal of religion and its practice, if it becomes a privatized pursuit, natural reconfigurations can nevertheless sustain a vital sense of religion.

In *After Rorty*, I describe what I called "edifying theology."[79] I described mostly the ethical element of theological language after Rorty's critique of first philosophy. I'd like to continue the discussion, charting out edifying theology more fully as a religious, privatized pursuit of perfection. As with other private pursuits, there is no obligation for others to follow it, nor does it prescribe a path for others. It is not even unique as a general approach to religion and religious belief, but it is how I envision it for myself within my own personal narrative.

Consider religion not in its institutional forms, with its centuries-long accumulation of history and doctrine, but in the context of our understanding of human evolution, as an original impulse arising in early humanity as a means of trying to navigate through and understand the natural environment, both the violent and grand events of nature. The genesis of the religious impulse is in the awe our early ancestors would have felt gazing at the oceans, mountains, moon, sun, and stars. This is religion at its emergence as a response to our conscious awakening with nature. It is the source of religion described by various scholars of religion, but most profoundly by Rudolf Otto, Mircea Eliade, and Peter Berger.

Otto, in his seminal study *The Idea of the Holy*, described the genesis of the religious impulse this way:

> 'Religious dread' (or 'awe') [in its] antecedent stage is 'daemonic dread' (cf. the horror of Pan) with its queer perversion, a sort of abortive offshoot, the 'dread of ghosts'. It first begins to stir in the feeling of 'something uncanny', 'eerie', or 'weird'. It is this feeling which, emerging in the mind of primeval man, *forms the starting-point for the entire religious development in history.* 'Daemons' and 'gods' alike spring from this root, and all the products of 'mythological apperception' or 'fantasy' are nothing but different modes in which it has been objectified. And all ostensible explanations of the origin of religion in terms of animism or magic or folk psychology are doomed from the outset to wander astray and miss the real goal of their inquiry, unless they recognize this fact of our nature—primary, unique, underivable from anything else—to be the basic factor and the basic impulse underlying the entire process of religious evolution.[80]

Eliade argued similarly. As a historian of religion his "ultimate aim" in his landmark study was "to understand, and to make understandable to others, religious man's behavior and mental universe." As a consequence, and as good advice for those who only examine religion in its historical or contemporary institutional forms, Eliade stressed that this approach, even in the "religious vision of classical antiquity . . . does not yet suffice for a comprehension of the mental universe of *homo religiosus*." Instead, "to come to know the mental universe of *homo religiosus*, we must above all take into account the men of these primitive societies." An existential hermeneutics on the part of the inquirer is required. "There is no other way of understanding a foreign mental universe than to place oneself *inside* it, at its very center, in order to progress from there to all the values that it possesses."[81]

Eliade's advice for an existential hermeneutics holds generally when we are trying to understand someone else's worldview, primitive, contemporary, and everything in between. But there is no obligation for others to attempt this understanding with private pursuits. With a private "religious experience," because there is no claim to Truth, there is no proselytizing, and so there is no interest on my part that others also pursue it. Otto can then be read as tempering Eliade's advice when he says:

> The reader is invited to direct his mind to a moment of deeply-felt religious experience, as little as possible qualified by other forms of consciousness. Whoever cannot do this, whoever knows no such moments in his experience, is requested to read no farther; for it is not easy to discuss questions of religious psychology with one who can recollect the emotions of his adolescence, the discomforts of indigestion, or, say, social feelings, but cannot recall any intrinsically religious feelings.[82]

Intrinsic or not (I'm not sure what that means), reflecting upon religious feelings, as with other private pursuits, is a useless task unless there some sort of interest in doing so. While we might be able to make the argument that acquiring a new skill or new insight into a topic will add to our overall character, trying to persuade others to do so because they will become the right kind of person is wrongheaded.[83]

Otto and Eliade describe these religious impulses, experiences, and feelings as part of our "existential situation," where "*experiences* and not simply *ideas*" are expressed. "The existence of *homo religiosus*," Eliade continues, "especially of the primitive, is open to the world; in living, religious man is never alone, part of the world lives in him."[84] Peter Berger, not a historian of religion but a scholar interested in religion as a sociological phenomenon, in *The Sacred Canopy*, offers a compatible sense of religion:

> The sacred is apprehended as "sticking out" from the normal routines of everyday life.... Religion implies the farthest reach of man's self-externalization, of his infusion of reality with his own meaning. Religion implies that human order is projected into the totality of being. Put differently, religion is the audacious attempt to conceive of the entire universe as being humanly significant.[85]

As with other aesthetic, private experiences, whether music, art, literature or poetry, our sense of *awe and wonder* (which is also compatible with a naturalist, evolutionist view of human biology) can take us beyond ourselves. If we take this original impulse as the opening to a sense of religion we can have today in post-Christian, post-philosophical culture, this sense cannot be what it was in its earliest expressions, "an absolute reality, [the] *the sacred*, which transcends this world but manifests itself in this world, thereby sanctifying it and making it real."[86] The awe is not some key to discovering "otherworldly" meaning but rather the astonishment shared in our quantum, biological, and physical commonality with the universe of things. Sounding much like Rorty and Vattimo, Berger emphasizes that whatever meaning we derive from this feeling, even what is classically described as a "religious experience," "will have to be rigorously bracketed." Our interpretations "are only available as meaning-enclaves within *this* world, the world of human experience in nature and history. As such, they must be analyzed as are all other human meanings, that is, as elements of the socially constructed world."[87] Or, as Rorty himself noted, whether from science, philosophy, religion, or poetry, "none of the words human beings have invented to describe themselves and their environment enjoy a special relation to reality."[88] Each of these disciplines is a fallibilist account.

Deciphering this sentiment, if we choose to call it the sacred, is a hermeneutical, not metaphysical undertaking. An integral part of the hermeneutical project is the use of the human imagination. Religious imagining, in contrast to religious metaphysics, *imagines* whether there is a God; whether there is an afterworld; whether there is something beyond the physical, wondering how we can explain the love we have for a child or the abject grief at the passing of a loved one. Because this exercise is part of the human capacity for imagining and not the metaphysical project of the human mind piercing reality, the imagination that finds itself captivated by this "sticking-out" doesn't make strong truth claims that this religious impulse is "hard-wired into all human organisms" and "basic to human nature,"[89] that God must exist, that there is life after death, and that there is a spiritual realm. The way we survey our beliefs and thoughts could be otherwise; can we imagine God not existing? That death is the end of consciousness? That there is nothing beyond the natural world, the here and now? Similarly, religious imagining, just like ordinary imagining, considers the awe we sense looking at the splendor of sunsets, stars, and oceans, but perhaps this awe is our mind reeling in the common origins that we have with the universe around us. Secularity, along with its own investigations into the origins of life, our world, and the universe, also offers a way of understanding not as natural revelation—God showing himself through the splendor of nature—but by our very human, scientific explanations.[90] With its various qualifications and possible alternative accounts fully entertained by our minds, the religious imagination shouldn't be thought of as false or a delusion. Rorty himself refers to senses of poetry and religion as "human creations and none the worse for that." In religious terms, believing that this impulse is fully explainable otherwise, is where faith resides. Faith is not holding to something tenaciously in spite of all explanations to the contrary.

Having left Christian fundamentalism as a graduate student over twenty-five years ago, the way I imagine many religious themes, still finds a certain reverberation in the stories, imagery, myth, symbolism, and archetypes of Christianity and the Bible.[91] While I no longer have any interest in attending church, I read the Bible as wisdom literature, though not as a door into the mind of God nor a dictated, thorough account of what we should believe historically or think scientifically or how we should act morally. As wisdom literature, it is neither inerrant nor infallible. Its intent is rather to speak to the human condition, giving fodder to the imagination. As a consequence, if it is read as an altogether historical, scientific, factual, prescriptive account of reality, it will sound like nonsense, imposing "on the faithful the burden of having to endure the secularization of knowledge and the pluralism of world pictures regardless of the religious truths they hold."[92]

Instead, as with investigations into other bodies of literature, religious, philosophical, political, scientific, or otherwise, reading the Bible is also a hermeneutical process: "it means recognizing that something is better understood the more one is able to say about it."[93] This is the main virtue of Richard Rorty's writings—that we are now able to say much more about philosophy, religion, and religious belief.

NOTES

1   G. Elijah Dann, *After Rorty: The Possibilities for Ethics and Religious Belief* (London: Continuum Press, 2006). Although my main interest is how

Rorty's metaphilosophical analysis applies to Christianity, his critique also applies to other religions that use robust metaphysical terms and esoteric language, including talk about Reality and what is True.

2 Richard Rorty and Gianni Vattimo, *The Future of Religion*, ed. Santiago Zabala (New York: Columbia University Press, 2005).

3 This isn't to say that their collective criticisms against the Church and religious belief does not have some merit. There's merit, but showing where it is, is quite beside the point in my example.

4 See Richard Rorty, *Achieving Our Country* (Cambridge, Mass.: Harvard University Press, 1998). For an impressive account of Rorty's intellectual development, see Neil Gross, *Richard Rorty: The Making of an American Philosopher* (Chicago: University of Chicago Press, 2008).

5 Robert Harrison's interview with Richard Rorty in 2005 is a lucid discussion of Rorty's metaphilosophical views. See "Richard Rorty—a Conversation," an interview by Robert Harrison, *Entitled Opinions*, 22 November 2005, Stanford University, iTunes U.

6 In *Philosophy and the Mirror of Nature* (Princeton, N.J.: Princeton University Press, 1979), Rorty distinguishes between "Philosophy" as first philosophy, and "philosophy" as pursuing solutions to the problems of humanity.

7 Richard Rorty, *Philosophy and Social Hope* (New York: Penguin Press, 1999), 150.

8 Rorty, *Philosophy and the Mirror of Nature*, 168–69. Jaegwon Kim describes philosophy, as epistemology, as setting *"universal standards of rationality and objectivity* for all actual and possible claims to knowledge" ("Rorty on the Possibility of Philosophy," *The Journal of Philosophy* 77, no. 10 [1980]: 590; emphasis his).

9 In contrast, pragmatists "do not accept the Cartesian-Kantian picture presupposed by the idea of 'our minds' or 'our language' as an 'inside' which can be contrasted to something (perhaps something very different) 'outside'" (Richard Rorty, *Objectivity, Relativism, and Truth* [Cambridge: Cambridge University Press, 1991], 12).

10 Rorty, *Philosophy and Social Hope*, 151.

11 Rorty quipped that "How real are our beliefs?" is a question that nobody would ask "unless he had some invidious contrast in mind between things that are *really* real and things that are (as Royce put it) 'not so damned real'" (Richard Rorty, *Truth and Progress* [New York: Cambridge University Press, 1998],116–17; emphasis his).

12 Rorty, *Philosophy and the Mirror of Nature*, 3.

13 Richard Rorty, *Consequences of Pragmatism* (Minneapolis: University of Minnesota Press, 1982), 165; emphasis his. Commenting on the relationship between the words we use and the world around us, Rorty notes: "Given a language and a view of what the world is like, one can, to be sure, pair off bits of the language with bits of what one takes the world to be in such a way that the sentences one believes true have internal structures isomorphic to relations between things in the world. When we rap out routine undeliberated reports like 'This is water,' 'That's red,' 'That's ugly,' 'That's immoral,' our short categorical sentences can easily be thought of as pictures, or as symbols which fit together to make a map. Such reports do indeed pair little bits of language with little bits of the world. . . . The great fallacy of the tradition, the pragmatists tell us, is to think that the metaphors of vision, correspondence, mapping, picturing, and representation which apply to small, routine assertions, will apply to large and debatable ones. This basic error begets the notion that where there are no objects to correspond to we have no hope of rationality, but only taste, passion, and will" (*Consequences of Pragmatism*, 162, 164).

14 Gabriel Vahanian, "The Denatured Nature of Ethics: In Praise of the Secular," *Philosophie de la religion entre éthique et ontologie*, comp. Marco M. Olivetta (Padua: Biblioteca dell' Archivio di Filosofia, Cedam, 1996), 508.

15 Vahanian, "The Denatured Nature of Ethics," 508.

16 Rorty, *Objectivity, Relativism, and Truth*, 37.

17 Rorty agrees with how Rawls explains his understanding of justice: "What justifies a conception of justice is not its being true to an order antecedent and given to us, but its congruence with our deeper understanding of

ourselves and our aspirations, and our realization that, given our history and the traditions embedded in our public life, it is the most reasonable doctrine for us" (John Rawls, "Kantian Constructivism in Moral Theory," *Journal of Philosophy* 77 [1980]: 519; quoted in Rorty, *Contingency, Irony, and Solidarity* [New York: Cambridge University Press, 1989], 58).

18 Rorty, *Consequences of Pragmatism*, xxv.

19 John Dewey, *Reconstruction in Philosophy* (New York: The New American Library, 1950), 156.

20 Rorty, *Philosophy and the Mirror of Nature*, 212.

21 Santiago Zabala also has it right when he comments that the "ultimate goal of philosophical investigation after the end of metaphysics is no longer contact with something existing independently from us, but rather *Bildung*, the unending formation of oneself" ("A Religion Without Theists or Atheists," in Richard Rorty and Gianni Vattimo, *The Future of Religion*, ed. Santiago Zabala [New York: Columbia University Press, 2005], 4). As we'll see below, this is compatible as well with religion after the end of metaphysics.

22 Rorty, *Philosophy and Social Hope*, 149. In *The Future of Religion*, Rorty mentions the desire by some to replace Habermas's communicative reason with "what Terry Pinkard calls 'Hegel's doctrine of the sociality of reason'" (30).

23 The recent discussion about Antony Flew's apparently shifting his belief from atheism to deism illustrates this tendency by evangelicals to think that the conversion of a well-known figure grants legitimacy to their religious faith. See Mark Oppenheimer, "The Turning of an Atheist," *New York Times Magazine*, 4 November 2007, http://www.nytimes.com/2007/11/04/magazine/04Flew-t.html. Supposed deathbed conversions are also of great interest to evangelicals because of the conversions' value as a technique for proselytizing. The most popular are Charles Darwin's and Betrand Russell's alleged—but altogether unlikely—changes of heart at the ends of their lives. The subtext is that if such a well-known thinker now believes in God, we Christians can rest comfortable in the

epistemological legitimacy of religious belief, and the rest of you skeptics should, too. Remembering my analogy at the beginning of this chapter, there is an interesting relationship between the sentiments surrounding a well-known person's religious conversion and the sentiments felt when a well-known member of a religious community abandons the faith. In either case, the sentiments, either positive or negative, come about because of the assumption that the belief or disbelief of others has a strong bearing on the legitimacy of one's own faith.

24 Richard Rorty, "Anticlericalism and Atheism," in Richard Rorty and Gianni Vattimo, *The Future of Religion*, ed. Santiago Zabala (New York: Columbia University Press, 2005), 33.

25 Martin Heidegger, *Identity and Difference*, trans. Joan Stambaugh (New York: Harper Torchbooks, 1966), 54.

26 Dewey, *Reconstruction in Philosophy*, 99–100.

27 Etienne Gilson, *God and Philosophy* (New Haven, Conn.: Yale University Press, 1941), 43. For a further discussion of the relationship between philosophy and Christian theology, see my chapter "Rorty and the Transformation of Theology," in *After Rorty*.

28 Jürgen Habermas, "Pre-political Foundations of the Democratic Constitutional State?" in Jürgen Habermas and Joseph Ratzinger, *The Dialectics of Secularization: On Reason and Religion* (San Francisco: Ignatius Press, 2006), 44.

29 Rorty, in his own writings, borrows this term from Hilary Putnam. See *Objectivity, Relativism, and Truth*, 6. Rorty adds, "But we have no idea what it would be like to be at that standpoint." Contrast this view with Thomas Nagel's, who thinks that "to deprive ourselves of such notions as 'representation' and 'correspondence' would be to stop 'trying to climb outside of our own minds, an effort some would regard as insane and that I regard as philosophically fundamental'" (Rorty, *Objectivity, Relativism, and Truth*, 7; quoting from Thomas Nagel, *The View from Nowhere* [New York: Oxford University Press, 1986], 11).

30 It is the desire "to extend the reference of 'us' as far as we can" (Rorty, *Objectivity, Relativism, and Truth*, 23). Kai Nielsen understands objectivity in the following terms: "We say that a morality or a set of moral views is justified ('objectively justified' if that isn't pleonastic) when, at a given time in a cool hour, among reasonable people properly informed, these people achieve a reflective consensus on what is to be done and on what moral views to hold." The advantage of defining objectivity in this manner is that it is an "utterly nonmetaphysical conception of objectivity compatible with reflective common sense ('critical commonsensism,' to use Peirce's phrase) and with an appeal to our considered judgments" (*After the Demise of the Tradition: Rorty, Critical Theory, and the Fate of Philosophy* [Oxford: Westview Press, 1991], 242–43).

31 Rorty, *Objectivity, Relativism, and Truth*, 24

32 Richard Rorty, "Pragmatism as Romantic Polytheism," in *The Revival of Pragmatism: New Essays on Social Thought, Law, and Culture*, ed. Morris Dickstein (Durham, N.C.: Duke University Press, 1998), 28.

33 See especially the contrast in Kai Nielsen's own writings between his highly philosophical critique of God talk in *Philosophy and Atheism: In Defense of Atheism* (New York: Prometheus Books, 1985), and his very sympathetic reading of Rorty in "Taking Rorty Seriously," *Dialogue* 38, no. 3 (1999): 503–18, as well as his *After the Demise of the Tradition*. I describe this inconsistency in "And Now, How About Taking God-Talk Seriously?" *International Journal for the Philosophy of Religion* 51 (2002): 101–9.

34 One of the most startling recent examples of this mindset was the 2008 Republican Party debates for the presidential nomination. The format of one particular debate, broadcast on CNN, was unique. The questions were selected from a number of submissions sent to CNN by way of YouTube. Off to the side of the auditorium there was a large screen where the chosen video clips were shown to the audience and candidates. Soon into the debate, there was a video offered by a young man from Texas. With a rather distant look in his eyes, this fellow posed his question to the can-

didates: "How you answer this question will tell us everything we need to know about you. Do you believe every word of this book?" At that point he held up to the camera a thick black book with "Holy Bible" emblazoned in gold on its cover. He then continued in a firm and steely voice: "And I mean specifically, this book that I am holding in my hand. *Do you believe this book?*" Unfortunately, but not unexpectedly, various candidates tried to respond in a favorable manner, knowing that it would be favorable to their nomination to do so.

35 Rorty, "Anticlericalism and Atheism," 33.

36 There are many more assumptions that lurk as well: God is interested in human affairs; that the Bible is his word (as opposed to the Koran or the Bhagavad Gita); and that the morality derived from the Bible was intended to be binding on all societies.

37 Stephen L. Carter, *The Culture of Disbelief: How American Law and Politics Trivialize Religious Devotion* (New York: BasicBooks, 1993), 171. See Rorty, "Religion as Conversation-Stopper," *Common Knowledge* 3, no. 1 (1994): 1–6, and his important follow-up article, "Religion in the Public Square: A Reconsideration," *Journal of Religious Ethics* 31, no. 1 (2003): 141–49.

38 Habermas, "Pre-political Foundations," 41–42.

39 Rorty, *Philosophy and Social Hope*, 149, 148.

40 Rorty, *Philosophy and Social Hope*, 170–71.

41 Rorty, "Anticlericalism and Atheism," 33.

42 Carter, *The Culture of Disbelief*; quoted in Rorty, *Philosophy and Social Hope*, 172.

43 Rorty, *Philosophy and Social Hope*, 173.

44 Rorty, "Richard Rorty—a Conversation."

45 Stout instead thinks that "reasons actually held in common do not get us far enough toward answers to enough of our political questions" (Jeffrey Stout, *Democracy and Tradition* [Princeton, N.J.: Princeton University Press, 2004], 89–90). This depends on what Stout thinks is the scope of "reasons held in common," and which "answers" we are looking to find.

In any case, it's unclear how Stout thinks we'll sort through our values in the public square if trying to work from a common set of basic values (for instance, that pleasure is better than torture, liberty better than confinement, and solidarity better than hatred) and reasons for holding them won't provide a good start. Beyond a large swath of basic moral and legal principles that we hold in common, there is also no need for us to ignore, holus bolus, the history of our Western tradition. We should, however, be ready to work through it whenever justified challenges arise.

46 Jürgen Habermas, *The Future of Human Nature* (New York: Polity, 2003), 109.

47 Rorty, *Philosophy and Social Hope*, 173–74.

48 Epithets from Dawkins, Hitchens, Dennett, and Harris, respectively.

49 Mircea Eliade and Habermas, perhaps for different reasons, agreed that there would be a continuance of religious belief. For Eliade, "To whatever degree he may have desacralized the world, the man who has made his choice in favor of a profane life never succeeds in completely doing away with religious behavior" (*The Sacred and the Profane: The Nature of Religion*, trans. Willard R. Trask [Toronto: Harcourt, 1959], 23). For Habermas, "religion is holding its own in an increasingly secular environment and . . . society must assume that religious fellowships will continue to exist for the foreseeable future" ("Pre-political Foundations," 46). Concerning human nature, this is a point that Chris Hedges takes up in *I Don't Believe in Atheists* (New York: Free Press, 2008). In contrast, Rorty's view of human nature and social progress is, decidedly, of a more optimistic sort.

50 Rorty, "Anticlericalism and Atheism," 30–31.

51 Rorty, "Anticlericalism and Atheism," 33.

52 Originally published in *The Cambridge Companion to William James*, ed. Ruth Anna Putnam (Cambridge: Cambridge University Press, 1997). Republished in Rorty's *Philosophy and Social Hope*, 148–67.

53 Here Rorty quotes from William James, "The Will to Believe," in *The Will to Believe and Other Essays in Popular Philosophy* (Cambridge: Mass.: Harvard University Press, 1979), 148; from *Philosophy and Social Hope*, 148.

54 Rorty, *Philosophy and Social Hope*, 149.

55 Rorty, *Philosophy and Social Hope*, 148. I've expanded these five points in *After Rorty*, 67–74.

56 Rorty, "Anticlericalism and Atheism," 39. On the same page Rorty continues, "It may be, but it may not. There is still a big difference between people like myself and people like Vattimo. Considering that he was raised a Catholic and I was raised in no religion at all, this is not surprising."

57 Gianni Vattimo, *Belief*, trans. Luca D'Isanto and David Webb (Stanford, Calif.: Stanford University Press, 1999), 39; Vattimo, *After Christianity*, trans. Luca D'Isanto (New York: Columbia University Press, 2002).

58 Rorty, "Anticlericalism and Atheism," 35.

59 Rorty, "Anticlericalism and Atheism," 35.

60 Rorty, "Anticlericalism and Atheism," 34, quoting Vattimo, *Belief*, 21.

61 Compare with the New Testament passage Philippians 2:6–8.

62 Rorty, "Anticlericalism and Atheism," 40.

63 Gianni Vattimo, in Rorty, Vattimo, and Zabala, "Dialogue: What Is Religion's Future After Metaphysics?" in Rorty and Vattimo, *The Future of Religion*, ed. Zabala (New York: Columbia University Press, 2005), 66.

64 Gianni Vattimo, with Piergiorgio Paterlini, *Not Being God: A Collaborative Autobiography*, trans. William McCuaig (New York: Columbia University Press, 2009), 19. For an earlier, more extensive account of nonmetaphysical religiousness, see his *Belief*. For a further description of weak thought, see Vattimo, *After Christianity*.

65 Vattimo, *Not Being God*, 15. In the religious context, it is difficult to find a more profound explanation of how this "masking" takes place than in Peter Berger's landmark study, *The Sacred Canopy: Elements of a Sociological Theory of Religion* (New York: Anchor Books, 1990). See, especially, his first chapter, "Religion and World-Construction," 3–28. "Men," Berger declares, "are congenitally compelled to impose a meaningful order upon reality" (22).

66 Vattimo, *Not Being God*, 15, 17.

67 Vattimo, *Not Being God*, 17–18.

68 Vattimo, *Not Being God*, 18. Perhaps this sense of the death of God is compatible with Gabriel Vahanian's sense, described in his groundbreaking study, *The Death of God: The Culture of Our Post-Christian Era* (New York: George Braziller, 1961): "The essence of Christianity, in the highest hours of man's faith in God, manifested itself (in C. S. Lewis's words) in drawing man away from gossiping about God" (3).

69 Vattimo, *Not Being God*, 18–19.

70 Vattimo, *Not Being God*, 19.

71 Vattimo, *Not Being God*, 24. See D'Isanto's explanation of Vattimo's distinction between "reactive nihilism (one which sees the nullity of the world as a matter of oppression and pessimism), and active nihilism, one which joyfully—that is, without resentment—embraces the nullity of the world and reinvents itself artistically" (Luca D'Isanto, introduction to Gianni Vattimo, *Belief*, trans. Luca D'Isanto and David Webb [Stanford, Calif.: Stanford University Press, 1999], 4–5). For a further description of Vattimo's sense of nihilism, see his *Nihilism and Emancipation: Ethics, Politics, and Law*, ed. Santiago Zabala, trans. William McCuaig (New York: Columbia University Press, 2004). See Rorty's foreword to that volume for a further description of Nietzsche's and Heidegger's effects on traditional philosophy.

72 Vattimo, *Not Being God*, 24.

73 Solomon, *Spirituality for the Skeptic: The Thoughtful Love of Life* (Oxford: Oxford University Press, 2002), xii. For my review of this book see *The Review of Metaphysics* (September 2003). While Rorty's problematizing of the words central to traditional philosophy—words like truth, objectivity, rationality—is rejected by many professional philosophers, there are those who write about these subjects in a way that would irk Rorty, Solomon, and professional philosophers alike. Although Karen Armstrong's work should be praised for bringing a wide readership to the topics of religion, she describes her approach to religions, in *The Case for God* (Knopf, 2009): "discover[ing] their truth—or lack of it"; "to 'step outside' the prism of ego and experience the sacred" (xiii); religion, like music, brings

our minds "to elide naturally into an apprehension of transcendence . . . marking the 'limits of reason.' . . . Yet this intensely rational activity segues transcendence [but] confronts us with a mode of knowledge that defies logical analysis and empirical proof" (xiv). Finally, Armstrong notes her concern "that many people are confused about the nature of religious truth" (xvii). Rorty would say, among other things, that her language conveys the attempt to get in touch with something larger than ourselves, and so the confusion arises because we continue to talk about truth as being discovered and claim that there is something called a "rational activity." However, if a more traditional, philosophical understanding of these terms is what she has in mind, Rorty's critics would ask what Armstrong means by the word "knowledge," especially knowledge that claims content that "defies logical analysis and empirical proof"? Moreover, if we aren't engaging in mere word magic and citing platitudes, what is it, in particular, that we are apprehending about transcendence?

74 Solomon, *Spirituality for the Skeptic*, xiii; emphasis his. Solomon distinguished between religion and spirituality, but I think it's an unfortunate and all too popular stipulation. More colloquially it's often phrased, "I'm not religious but I consider myself very spiritual." This distinction has come about because of cultural forces, not etymological considerations. Like Solomon, those who are critical of organized religion want to assign all ascriptions to religion under this heading, and, in contrast, "spirituality" is used to refer to everything from Solomon's naturalized spirituality to various esoteric expressions of New Age theology. Etymologically, however, "religion" has no necessary association with institutional religious practice and can easily be a synonym for "spirituality."

75 Vattimo, *After Christianity*, 6.

76 Sue Roberts, "News: Souled Out," *Philosophy Now* (July/August 2009): 5.

77 See, for example, Douglas Farrow, ed., *Recognizing Religion in a Secular Society: Essays in Pluralism, Religion, and Public Policy* (Montreal: McGill-Queen's University Press, 2004).

78 Vattimo nevertheless admits that "while our civilization no longer explicitly professes itself Christian but rather considers itself by and large a dechristianized, post-Christian, lay civilization, it is nevertheless profoundly shaped by that heritage at its source" (*Belief*, 43).

79 See my *After Rorty*, 158.

80 Rudolf Otto, *The Idea of the Holy*, trans. John W. Harvey (New York: Oxford University Press, 1958), 14–15; emphasis mine.

81 Eliade, *The Sacred and the Profane*, 162–63, 165; emphasis his. Eliade is very conscious of the difficulty trying to do so, especially in contemporary society: "For our purpose it is enough to observe that desacralization pervades the entire experience of the nonreligious man of modern societies and that, in consequence, he finds it increasingly difficult to rediscover the existential dimensions of religious man in the archaic societies" (*The Sacred and the Profane*, 13).

82 Otto, *The Idea of the Holy*, 8.

83 Karen Armstrong comes close to arguing this way: "Religion is a practical discipline that teaches us to discover new capacities of mind and heart. . . . You will discover their truth—or lack of it—only if you translate these doctrines into ritual or ethical action. . . . But those who do not apply themselves will get nowhere at all" (*The Case for God*, xiii). Perhaps it is owing to my Christian fundamentalist background, but I find such encouragement very similar to the language of contemporary evangelicalism, predicated on the assumption that this is something that'll make you better. To the contrary, I've found religious belief to be a very familiar and comfortable pursuit. If you find yourself having to work too hard at it, perhaps just like other interests we may pick up but find we aren't very good at—it might not be for you—or, maybe it should be reserved, like a rainy-day hobby, for reading a book on religion in a cafe.

84 Eliade, *The Sacred and the Profane*, 166; emphasis his.

85 Berger, *The Sacred Canopy*, 26.

86 Eliade, *The Sacred and the Profane*, 202; emphasis his.

87 Berger, *The Sacred Canopy*, 88–89; emphasis his.

88 Richard Rorty, foreword to *Nihilism and Emancipation: Ethics, Politics, and Law*, by Gianni Vattimo, ed. Santiago Zabala, trans. William McCuaig (New York: Columbia University Press, 2004), xiii.

89 See Rorty, "Anticlericalism and Atheism," 39.

90 It's unfortunate that theologians of the Christian triumphalist persuasion still wish to argue that the awe we feel when looking at nature is "natural revelation"—God revealing his attributes through our observation of nature—supposing that this is the only possible interpretation of this feeling of awe. Undoubtedly because of our long, held resistance to evolution, we are only beginning, especially in North America, to come to grips with how an understanding of evolution now informs our other inquiries, such as morality and religion. An important recent study is Nicholas Wade, *The Faith Instinct: How Religion Evolved and Why It Endures* (New York: Penguin Press, 2009). For example, Wade describes how religion granted moral stability in early society: "Religion, above all, embodies the moral rules that members of a community observe toward one other [*sic*]. It thus sustains the quality of the social fabric, and did so alone in early societies that had not developed civil authorities. It binds people together for collective action, through public rituals that evoke emotional commitment to a common cause" (2). However, in today's secular and democratic society, we do have developed, nonreligious civil authorities and a decidedly pluralistic "social fabric" that informs us how we should pursue "collective action." As a result, contrary to what religious conservatives argue, religious morality served a very different purpose in the past and can't merely be transposed into today's society. Eliade reminds us that "nonreligious man descends from *homo religiosus* and, whether he likes it or not, he is also the work or religious man; his formation begins with the situations assumed by his ancestors. . . . In other words, profane man cannot help preserving some vestiges of the behavior of religious man, though they are emptied of religious meaning" (*The Sacred and the Profane*, 203–4).

91 Along with fourteen other contributors, I wrote about my time as a Christian fundamentalist and how I abandoned it in G. Elijah Dann, ed., *Leav-*

ing Fundamentalism: Personal Stories, foreword by Thomas Moore (Waterloo: Wilfrid Laurier Press, 2008).

92 Jürgen Habermas, "A Conversation About God and the World: An Interview with Eduardo Mendieta," trans. Max Pensky, in *Religion and Rationality: Essays on Reason, God, and Modernity*, ed. and intro. Eduardo Mendieta (Cambridge, Mass.: MIT Press, 2002), 151. If there is one element within the critique of religion by the new atheists that bears attention, it is that the Bible contains all sorts of vile, unjustifiable behavior—not only of the "wicked" but also of those called "righteous." The Bible certainly does ask us to help the poor, but it also has God telling his people to go into a neighboring tribe to kill everyone, women and children included. If we wish to argue that the Bible provides our basis for morality, how do we distinguish between scriptural commands we would all consider moral—such as having a concern for the poor—and other claims that even Christians no longer consider binding, such as having slaves and treating women like chattel? In "Religion in the Public Square: A Reconsideration," Rorty poses this very question to Nicholas Wolterstorff.

93 Zabala, "A Religion Without Theists or Atheists," 8.

BIBLIOGRAPHY

Armstrong, Karen. *The Case for God*. Toronto: Knopf, 2009.

Berger, Peter. *The Sacred Canopy: Elements of a Sociological Theory of Religion*. New York: Anchor Books, 1990.

Carter, Stephen L. *The Culture of Disbelief: How American Law and Politics Trivialize Religious Devotion*. New York: BasicBooks, 1993.

Dann, G. Elijah. *After Rorty: The Possibilities for Ethics and Religious Belief*. London & New York: Continuum Press, 2006.

——. "And Now, How About Taking God-Talk Seriously?" *International Journal for the Philosophy of Religion* 51 (2002): 101–9.

——, ed. *Leaving Fundamentalism: Personal Stories*. Foreword by Thomas Moore. Waterloo: Wilfrid Laurier Press, 2008.

Dewey, John. *Reconstruction in Philosophy*. New York: The New American Library, 1950.

D'Isanto, Luca. Introduction to *Belief*, by Gianni Vattimo, 1–17. Stanford, Calif.: Stanford University Press, 1999.

Eliade, Mircea. *The Sacred and the Profane: The Nature of Religion*. Trans. Willard R. Trask. Toronto: Harcourt, 1959.

Farrow, Douglas, ed. *Recognizing Religion in a Secular Society: Essays in Pluralism, Religion, and Public Policy*. Montreal: McGill-Queen's University Press, 2004.

Gilson, Etienne. *God and Philosophy*. New Haven, Conn.: Yale University Press, 1941.

Habermas, Jürgen. "A Conversation About God and the World: An Interview with Eduardo Mendieta." In *Religion and Rationality: Essays on Reason, God, and Modernity*, trans. Max Pensky. Ed. and intro. Eduardo Mendieta, 147–67. Cambridge, Mass.: The MIT Press, 2002.

——. *The Future of Human Nature*. New York: Polity, 2003.

——. "Pre-political Foundations of the Democratic Constitutional State?" In *The Dialectics of Secularization: On Reason and Religion*, by Jürgen Habermas and Joseph Ratzinger, 19–52. San Francisco: Ignatius Press, 2006.

Heidegger, Martin. *Identity and Difference*. Trans. Joan Stambaugh. New York: Harper Torchbooks, 1966.

Kim, Jaegwon. "Rorty on the Possibility of Philosophy." *The Journal of Philosophy* 77, no. 10 (1980): 589–90.

James, William. "The Will to Believe." In *The Will to Believe and Other Essays in Popular Philosophy*, 1–242. Cambridge: Mass.: Harvard University Press, 1979.

Nagel, Thomas. *The View from Nowhere*. New York: Oxford University Press, 1986.

Nielsen, Kai. *After the Demise of the Tradition: Rorty, Critical Theory, and the Fate of Philosophy.* Oxford: Westview Press, 1991.

——. *Philosophy and Atheism: In Defense of Atheism.* New York: Prometheus Books, 1985.

——. "Taking Rorty Seriously." *Dialogue* 38, no. 3 (1999): 503–18.

Oppenheimer, Mark. "The Turning of an Atheist." *New York Times Magazine*, 4 November 2007. http://www.nytimes.com/2007/11/04/magazine/04Flew-t.html. Accessed 1 February 2010.

Otto, Rudolf. *The Idea of the Holy.* Trans. John W. Harvey. New York: Oxford University Press, 1958.

Roberts, Sue. "News: Souled Out." *Philosophy Now* (July/August 2009).

Rorty, Richard. *Achieving Our Country.* Cambridge, Mass.: Harvard University Press, 1998.

——. "Anticlericalism and Atheism." In *The Future of Religion*, by Richard Rorty and Gianni Vattimo, ed. Santiago Zabala, 29–41. New York: Columbia University Press, 2005.

——. *Consequences of Pragmatism.* Minneapolis: University of Minnesota Press, 1982.

——. *Contingency, Irony, and Solidarity.* New York: Cambridge University Press, 1989.

——. Foreword to *Nihilism and Emancipation: Ethics, Politics, and Law*, by Gianni Vattimo, ed. Santiago Zabala, trans. William McCuaig, ix–xx. New York: Columbia University Press, 2004.

——. *Objectivity, Relativism, and Truth.* Cambridge: Cambridge University Press, 1991.

——. *Philosophy as Cultural Politics.* Cambridge: Cambridge University Press, 2007.

——. *Philosophy and Social Hope.* New York: Penguin Press, 1999.

——. *Philosophy and the Mirror of Nature.* Princeton, N.J.: Princeton University Press, 1979.

——. "Pragmatism as Romantic Polytheism." In *The Revival of Pragmatism: New Essays on Social Thought, Law, and Culture*, ed. Morris Dickstein, 21–36. Durham, N.C.: Duke University Press, 1998.

——. "Putnam and the Relativist Menace." *The Journal of Philosophy* 90, no. 9 (1993): 443–61.

——. "Religion as Conversation-Stopper." *Common Knowledge* 3, no. 1 (1994): 1–6.

——. "Religion in the Public Square: A Reconsideration." *Journal of Religious Ethics* 31, no. 1 (2003): 141–49.

——. "Richard Rorty—a Conversation." Interview by Robert Harrison. *Entitled Opinions*, 22 November 2005. Stanford University, iTunes U.

——. *Truth and Progress*. New York: Cambridge University Press, 1998.

——. *Truth, Politics, and 'Post-Modernism.'* Amsterdam: Van Gorcum, 1997.

Rorty, Richard, and Gianni Vattimo. *The Future of Religion*. Ed. Santiago Zabala. New York: Columbia University Press, 2005.

Solomon, Robert. *Spirituality for the Skeptic: The Thoughtful Love of Life*. Oxford: Oxford University Press, 2002.

Vahanian, Gabriel. *The Death of God: The Culture of Our Post-Christian Era*. New York: George Braziller, 1961.

——. "The Denatured Nature of Ethics: In Praise of the Secular." In *Philosophie de la religion entre éthique et ontologie*, comp. Marco M. Olivetta. Padua: Biblioteca dell' Archivio di Filosofia, Cedam, 1996.

Vattimo, Gianni. *After Christianity*. Trans. Luca D'Isanto. New York: Columbia University Press, 2002.

——. *Belief*. Trans. Luca D'Isanto and David Webb. Stanford, Calif.: Stanford University Press, 1999.

——. "Dialogue: What Is Religion's Future After Metaphysics?" In *The Future of Religion*, by Richard Rorty and Gianni Vattimo, ed. Santiago Zabala, 55–81. New York: Columbia University Press, 2005.

——. *Nihilism and Emancipation: Ethics, Politics, and Law*. Ed. Santiago Zabala, trans. William McCuaig. New York: Columbia University Press, 2004.

Vattimo, Gianni, with Piergiorgio Paterlini. *Not Being God: A Collaborative Autobiography*. Trans. William McCuaig. New York: Columbia University Press, 2009.

Wade, Nicholas. *The Faith Instinct: How Religion Evolved and Why It Endures*. New York: Penguin Press, 2009.

Zabala, Santiago, ed. "A Religion Without Theists or Atheists." In *The Future of Religion*, by Richard Rorty and Gianni Vattimo, ed. Santiago Zabala, 1–27. New York: Columbia University Press, 2005.